Mind Y

Venugopal Acharya is a full-time teacher, monk and counsellor at ISKCON. Before choosing the monastic order twenty years ago, he worked in the corporate sector, having earned an MBA in finance and a master's degree in international finance. He is a seasoned international speaker and has addressed audiences in the United Kingdom, Russia, Netherlands, Switzerland, Bahrain and Australia, sharing his thoughts on mental hygiene, emotional fulfilment and spiritual discipline.

He is author of *Are You Connected?* and *Cricket in a Monastery*. His daily blog is available at www.yogaformodernage.com

Mind Your Mind

Three Principles for
Happy Living

VENUGOPAL ACHARYA

hachette
INDIA

First published in India in 2020 by Hachette India
(Registered name: Hachette Book Publishing India Pvt. Ltd)
An Hachette UK company
www.hachetteindia.com

SRD

ISBN 978-93-89253-14-6

Hachette Book Publishing India Pvt. Ltd
4th & 5th Floors, Corporate Centre,
Plot No. 94, Sector 44, Gurugram – 122003, India

Typeset in Adobe Garamond Pro
by Jojy Philip, New Delhi – 15

Printed and bound in India by
Manipal Technologies Limited, Manipal

MIX
Paper from
responsible sources
FSC
www.fsc.org   FSC® C043100

To my parents and grandparents
Your love helps me live with my mind happily

Contents

Section 2: Acceptance

Section 3: Aspiration

Practical Application

Preface

I USED TO TEACH a weekly class on the Bhagavad Gita to young professionals in a Mumbai suburb. This was one of the services I had to offer as an ISKCON teacher–monk. One day, after my class had finished, about a dozen young men and women gathered around me to ask questions. Thirty-year-old Jaimit asked, 'Does your mind wander? Are you ever troubled by the capricious and unpredictable nature of the mind?'

'Yes, quite often,' I replied matter-of-factly.

'Oh,' he said, and fell silent.

I sensed his confusion. I knew he was thinking that if I was troubled myself, how could I speak to others on self-awareness and techniques to keep the mind peaceful?

'Our happiness or success in our various endeavours is not in controlling the mind,' I said, in an attempt to ease his discomfiture. 'We need to be more aware, that's all.'

A relieved smile lit up his face. 'Yes, that makes sense,' he said. 'Manager, manage your mind! I often feel hopeless because the mind is too difficult to control.'

'Difficult?' Sruti, his expressive wife, said, frowning. 'I think it's next to impossible to control the wild mind.'

'C'mon, yaar, it's not impossible; see our teacher here,' Vedant, a friend of Jaimit, chipped in, pointing to me.

Sruti looked at him and then back at me. She appeared unsure. Slowly, she nodded, as if to say, 'You are a lucky man; poor me, I am suffering!'

The others nodded in approval. I felt nervous realizing that the group hoped I could lead them in their attempts to gain control over their inner lives.

Many who attend my lectures are searching for happiness or at least some clues to figure out what to do with the wayward mind. I can often feel their desperation. *Do you have some tools that will help me keep my damned mind peaceful,* is the silent scream I hear from so many people I meet.

On this day, my students were distracted and restless, and I shuddered at the prospect of being their messiah. In fact, I saw *myself* as a seeker and spiritual practitioner rather than a self-realized soul. But I knew my students needed help and clarity. 'No, I haven't controlled my mind,' I said firmly. 'Nor do I want to.'

They gaped at me in disbelief.

'I'd prefer to accept myself the way I am, and then focus on cultivating life-enhancing principles; I want to be more attentive and present in my activities,' I said slowly. 'If you are aware and attentive, and accept yourself the way you are, then life is far more peaceful.'

I now had their full attention.

'Look, Sruti is talking to us, but she is aware of what Chinu is doing at the same time.' I pointed to her four-year-old daughter, who was playing with the other kids in the garden outside.

'The mother is present in our conversation, but she is also aware her child is elsewhere. So she has made a mental boundary within which Chinu can play. Once the little one moves outside the safety "zone" in any way, the mother will forget our discussion and rush to Chinu. Likewise, my mind is constantly restless, and I really can't do anything about it. I let the mind's tape play in the background, while I busy myself with what I am supposed to do. The mind is, after all, like an unreasonable, restless child, except that it never sleeps; nor does it give me respite. So I improve my awareness of the mind and watch out for its mischief, and it is capable of creating plenty of that!

'Does that make sense?' I now sought Sruti's endorsement.

She smiled broadly, the sceptic within her pacified.

Another young man added, 'We know we need to be more aware and more attentive. There are so many seminars on mindfulness; yet, why do we find it difficult to follow all that we learn?'

'I would say that it is because we often miss out on a vital part of the puzzle. Without that piece, the puzzle remains incomplete. Let me explain what I mean. Along with "Awareness" and "Acceptance", we need the third "A" in place – Aspiration, which complements the other two qualities.

'Let's briefly acquaint ourselves with each of these principles. If you are angry at someone, you are compelled to say or do something that you may later regret. If, however, you realize in the midst of that heated emotion that you are losing control of yourself, you have instantly risen above your mind. You are now aware of what is taking place within you.

'With improved awareness comes the second principle – acceptance – to help you deal with yourself. The negative self-talk, provoked by the ever-dissatisfied mind, can be countered with self-acceptance and by choosing principles that help us bring light to this world.

'And if your aspirations – the third principle – are aligned to universal values, if your intent is in harmony with the larger good of the society, it is likely you will safely sail through an emotionally charged situation.'

'Easier said than done,' Sruti said, the cynic in her getting the better of her again.

'Not really!' I responded. "Practice maketh a man – and a woman – perfect" is an old adage. A few easy-to-follow techniques that you could practise anywhere will surely help you improve your alertness to the mind's wanderings.'

We spoke for some more time and resolved to discover our true aspirations. We committed to increasing and improving our self-awareness and attention techniques, as well as to learning to accept ourselves the way we were.

The following week, Sruti and Jaimit came back and said they liked the techniques we discussed, and Sruti, in particular, looked happier and more hopeful.

That's when Jaimit suggested that I present these principles in a book that could help others as well. The sparkle in his eyes convinced me that he had benefitted from them. I instantly agreed. And that's how this book came to be written.

This book is my humble attempt to explain the three principles of mind management: Awareness, Acceptance and Aspiration.

When hassled by my mind, I remember my spiritual master, Radhanath Swami's golden words, 'Life is simple for the simple, complicated for the complicated.'

The mind is a simple phenomenon as well, and even if psychologists and neuroscientists disagree, I have presented the concept of the mind simply, in layman's language.

The book is not an academic presentation; instead, through a mixture of anecdotes and experiences from my own monastic life, and also using some historical events and news from around the world, I have shared the technique of mind management to help you face your life's daily challenges with clarity and ease.

Most of the quotes from the Bhagavad Gita are from the edition by Bhaktivedanta Swami.

I pray and hope this book benefits you, the reader. I seek your blessings and pray that I can serve you.

VENUGOPAL ACHARYA

Introduction

'EXCUSE ME,' I YELLED. I was in a state of panic, and my words came out with difficulty. 'Do man-eating tigers roam around here?'

A little distance away, I had just spotted a man who seemed to be about seventy years old. He turned towards me, a dreamy look on his face. How could he remain unruffled while wandering alone in this lonely and dangerous forest?

'Hmm…' he murmured as he lazily picked up twigs from the forest floor.

I could not understand his behaviour. Dissonant sounds rang through the forest. I recognized cuckoos, crickets, squirrels, monkeys and maybe a woodpecker's song, but most of the sounds were foreign to me. The forest itself appeared strange and foreboding. A sudden gust of wind had the trees swinging erratically. Giant fig trees and verdant bushes sent a chill through my spine because I thought perhaps a lion was prowling behind them.

'You are sweating,' the man observed nonchalantly. The predawn hours of the winter were biting cold, yet I was perspiring profusely.

'Yeah…no…er…I mean,' I fumbled. 'I heard there are tigers or lions here. Is it true?'

'I am not deaf,' he said.

'Oh sorry!' I hadn't realized that my voice had risen again in fear.

I used to walk for two hours daily before sunrise at the Sanjay Gandhi National Park in Borivali on the outskirts of northern Mumbai. Today was no different until I suddenly remembered a friend's casual remark a few days ago. When I had told him I was going for these walks, he mentioned that there were leopards and tigers in the forest. He was amused to hear that I walked alone every morning. He even suggested in passing that I carry a stick with me or, better still, wait for sunrise before I ventured into the jungle. However, we had spoken of many things that evening and I had forgotten about this discussion, until this morning.

At a particularly dark ridge on the eastern side of the woods, I had just spotted a flock of deer scamper. The branches of the trees shook violently and birds frantically flapped their wings. In an instant, the stillness was broken. I was gripped by a sudden terror, and snippets of that conversation with my friend came rushing back to me. I wondered desperately if there was a dangerous animal about. I was all alone, and had absolutely no way to protect myself.

Ironically, the previous evening, I had presented a seminar called 'Overcoming Fear', at which I had delineated systematic steps to tame the wild mind. Eight hours later, I stood exposed: I didn't remember a word of my talk. I didn't even know who I was or where I was. All I wanted to do was turn around and run; my 'flight' response was fully activated!

Here I was – a preacher and a monk – well known to members of the community, to which I delivered discourses on the mind, soul and God. But, at this moment, all I could think of was how I was going to become some tiger's meal. I looked at a giant tree nearby and wondered if I could climb it for safety. But what if there was a snake coiled in its branches?

Years ago, I had read in the papers that a lion had escaped from the park and attacked a few people before he was caught. I had not thought about that incident all this while. Now, I was convinced that a lion, apart from a tiger and snake, was also lurking nearby.

It was at this point that I ran into the old man. Oddly enough, he seemed at home here, even as I felt the sword of death dangling over my head.

After hearing my terrified questions, he looked at my saffron robes and his eyes widened. 'Oh, you are a swami!' he said. 'Yes, there are tigers and leopards here.' Then, with a dismissive wave of his hand, he said, 'You needn't worry, though. After all, you are a monk. They won't do anything to you.'

I gulped. 'How will a tiger know the difference between a monk and someone else, and why will he forsake a good meal? Do tigers respect holy men?' I tried being sarcastic, but my fear was palpable.

'Oh, son, you clearly don't know the rules of the jungle,' the old man said. 'The animals see saffron or red and immediately think it is fire. They stay away. That's why the holy men who once lived in the forests wore red cloth. But if you are in the ocean, avoid red. The sharks will mistake it for blood and attack you immediately, even if they are hundreds of miles away.'

I felt relieved and reassured that the tigers wouldn't get me; after all, this wise old man knew better than me the ways of the forest. And he was confident I was safe here. Still, I decided not to take any chances and hastily began my journey out of the forest. Mercifully, the sun rose bright and eventually the sight of other morning walkers with their long sticks gave me some relief.

THINKING ABOUT OUR THOUGHTS

This incident changed the way I thought about my thoughts.

After I returned from the forest, I sat alone feeling quite dazed, trying to comprehend what had happened to me that morning, trying to make sense of the way I had reacted.

It occurred to me with some shock how little I knew about my own mind. I still had fears. And I could not control my thoughts. I had learnt first-hand that there was a huge gap between the theory I preached from the scriptures and what I had actually internalized. I wasn't walking my own talk.

I realized that, so far, I had been seeing the world *through* my mind. That day, thanks to the experience in the forest, I took a step back within my internal world and actually observed how my mind *functioned*. Till now, I had analysed others with the help of the mind. But now, suddenly, I had some awareness of my own mind.

The old man in the forest had held up a mirror to my emotional and mental state. We often feel different emotions like love, anger, fear, etc. But when you are *aware* of your feelings, rather than simply feeling them, you have taken a step back within yourself and become an observer to your thoughts. For example, you could be fearful on a dark night. But if you could recognize at that moment that your mind is feeling fear, or if you could see yourself as separate from the emotion you're experiencing, you have risen above the mind.

This is the first step in the attempt to transform the mind into a friend.

◎◎

My experience in the forest changed me at a deeper level, for it triggered off my second innings as a monk.

Now, if a spiritual saying impressed me, I paused to consider whether it had merely pleased my mind and senses or penetrated deeper – had it touched my inner self?

I began to spend more time with myself. I was full of questions that had not occurred to me before, for example: Why is it that my mind does not listen to me but makes me follow its commands? Can I quell the constant and often confusing thoughts that arise in the mind? Is it possible to get this fickle mind to cooperate with me? Is the mind a friend of the self or an enemy out to destroy one's sense of peace? And, finally, I began to wonder about the big question: Is there more to me than my mind?

THREE PRINCIPLES TO MIND YOUR MIND

In the past, I'd often tell my friends that I was ordinary. I thought I was being modest and gracious when showered with praise. That morning in the forest, however, I had a rude awakening: I *knew* I was ordinary.

But was I ready to 'accept' this sudden 'awareness' that I was an average person filled with insecurities and fears?

It took me a few months of prayer and introspection to come to terms with who I really am. But when I did accept my frailties and made peace with myself, I felt like a free bird. I caused a slight shock in one of my classes when I confessed to the audience that I was a monk by accident, and that I had the same aspirations and need for emotional support as they did. Nonetheless, I had made the choice of being single, and was happily paying the price and enjoying the rewards of this choice. I knew that day that the secret to a life of contentment and freedom was in the honest 'acceptance of the self.'

I realized that awareness (of who we are) is a divine gift we receive when we live by sattva, a life of goodness centred on habits and thoughts that are conducive to improving awareness. I shall elaborate on this in Chapter 2 of the first section.

'Acceptance', however, is a choice – it is our willingness to accept being tiny in this giant cosmos, to feel humble and insignificant, yet loved by the Universe and God.

The real challenge is to *sustain* this feeling of humility, and that's when the third principle comes into play.

The mind is craftier than we can imagine. While awareness requires us to spend solitary moments with ourselves in order to understand the self, acceptance calls for humility. Yet, the problem isn't solved there! Even if we choose to be humble and have taken that decision, the mind will find ways to trick us again.

Despite the work I began to do on myself after my experience in the forest – and I have shared this with you briefly – it didn't take long for me to forget my humble existence and begin judging others once again. I would talk about things that I now considered small or meaningless, but knowing these things then made me feel superior to others. I thought I was better than them since I had understood the folly of the ego. For example, I would speak on pride and humility, but I did not realize that I was still full of myself. My guru, Radhanath Swami, often says, 'The proud man may behave humbly, but he will be proud of it.' And, therefore, that humility is a false one.

So what is the way out? How do we stay grounded? The only way is to connect to a noble *aspiration*, the third and the most important principle. I had to gently remind myself about my purpose in life by asking myself this: Why am I doing what I am doing? The moment I ask myself this question, I rise to a cause bigger than the mind's petty complaints. I now have an aspiration, and it is this aspiration that helps me face the mind's mood swings better. Seen from a higher standpoint, my mind's non-issues dissolved when I asked myself this question. American life coach Tony Robins calls this the 'Daily Priming' technique, where you connect to your goals for 10 minutes each morning so that you have a richer and more fulfilling cause to live for.

And this, in brief, is how we apply the three principles of Awareness, Acceptance and Aspiration to ourselves and our lives. This book explores the possibility of tapping the hidden powers of the mind through these three principles. The benefits you will receive will be immediate, and lasting.

Summing up the three principles, *Awareness* is the cognizance of what's happening now within you; *Acceptance* is letting go of the resistance – the fight – and staying in the present moment fully, without any guilt and fear; and *Aspiration* means to seek a larger goal in life, something much deeper and wider that just achieving our daily to-do lists.

Despite the mind's unruly and fickle nature, it is never too late to change, to regain control over our lives. If we can learn things we can practise daily to improve our awareness, acceptance and aspirations – acts that can be ingrained as habits – we'll be able to live genuinely happy lives. Besides, if we can acknowledge the lessons life teaches us, where humiliation often comes before we can learn to embrace humility, we will be able to stay aligned with our mission and be at peace with the mind. In fact, the cooperative mind could take us to unimaginable heights in our inner and outer lives.

THE FORMAT OF THE BOOK

The book is divided into three sections, each looking at the key principles I have been talking about. Within each section, there are chapters that can be read independently, if you so wish, or as a whole in order to understand that concept. For example, the first chapter in Section 1 gives us knowledge of the mind–ego–intelligence nexus. This leads us to understand the three energies that influence this trio, which you will learn about in the second chapter. This then raises a question about how we can manipulate positive energies to our advantage, which is the subject of Chapter 3. Like this, a total of 13 chapters help us learn Awareness. The Acceptance section has 14 chapters and Aspiration contains 11 chapters.

A summary follows each of the 38 chapters to help you remember the key takeaways.

One principle also connects with another. For instance, Acceptance includes overcoming guilt and developing self-love. Self-love that is distinguished from false pride happens only with improved self-awareness. Therefore, Awareness and Acceptance go together.

In fact, by now you must have understood that all three principles are interrelated, and it is not advisable to study or practise them individually. Only when the three of them come together are you able to apply these simple yet profound principles of mind management to change your life. Integrating the three principles is the real secret, and our daily spiritual practice helps us see the harmony and beauty of these principles in union.

It may also happen that you find essays in one of the sections more relevant than essays in another section of the book. Do not worry about that because, finally, all these keys merge.

My attempt to explain the dynamics of the mind, however, is fraught with limitations because I am an ordinary being, and can't claim to know everything about the mind. Still, my desire to serve and share is sincere. To be honest, I have written this book for three reasons: To educate myself; to serve you; and to please my beloved Lord.

Although life is not an easy journey and mere techniques can't resolve its deeper issues, the principles discussed in this book are meant to be like a torchlight – they'll likely help you discover your own techniques. You will be able to find your own methods and answers to the situations in *your* life. I assure you that if read with an open mind, these articles will open new frontiers of freedom. Moreover, you will definitely discover you are more than your mind.

A NOTE TO THE READER

Psychologists often refer to the highly complex cognitive process – or the inner language of thoughts, analysis, worries, hopes, perceptions, or our ability to recognize awareness – as the mind.

Although the mind is a complex subject matter, I have chosen to simplify things by treating it as an individual at some places in the book. Elsewhere in these pages, I have presented the mind as a thing that exists inside of us to help us think or feel. Along with the intelligence and ego, the mind remains one of the most fascinating subjects of study by psychologists as well as spiritual teachers.

This book is not a substitute for professional counselling or medical intervention; rather, it shares traditional spiritual wisdom that you can apply to the modern context. The book aims at improving your daily habits and thereby your overall well-being. For specific emotional challenges, it is advisable to see a therapist.

Since the purpose of this book is to improve Awareness, Acceptance and Aspiration, the concept of the mind is presented simply and non-academically. This does not in any way undermine the enormous contribution of science and psychology.

In *Mind Your Mind*, I share anecdotes and stories to drive home the need to improve Awareness, Acceptance, and Aspiration – the three As of effective mind management and happy living.

SECTION 1

Awareness

'For him, who has conquered the mind, the mind is the best of friends; but for one who has failed to do so, his mind will remain the greatest enemy.'

— Bhagavad Gita (6.6)

CHAPTER ONE

'Ego–Mind–Intelligence': Know the Lethal Gang

'The self, baffled by false ego thinks of himself as a doer.'
— Bhagavad Gita (3.27)

HAVE YOU EVER FELT positive feelings for someone on one occasion but, on another, found yourself feeling intense irritation or anger towards him? Did you believe a certain person to be your friend and trust her implicitly, yet come to a point where you suddenly found yourself unsure about your relationship with her?

If this happens to you frequently, you could be a victim of your mind's constant 'assaults'. Yes, within you, there's a criminal trio on the prowl. The members of this vicious mafia are Ego, Mind and Intelligence. Who are these three villains? What is their nexus and how do they operate?

Ego is a deep, false identity of the self; the one who drives the mind and intelligence to action.

Mind has the simple function of accepting or rejecting things.

Intelligence justifies this acceptance or rejection with arguments, logic and analysis.

EGO AND MIND IN ACTION

Ego is the boss, and controls both Intelligence and Mind. His diktat to you may sound like this: 'I am the enjoyer' or 'I am the greatest' or 'I deserve all respect and honour'.

Mind is a dutiful servant and Ego's bodyguard. He does only two things – accept or reject the statement that Ego makes.

Imagine an educated man with a degree from Harvard University and 30 years of experience in the corporate world. He comes along and compliments you for being a thoughtful and intelligent person.

What happens inside you then is that the 'boss', Ego, is happy: 'My estimation of myself being the greatest or being most deserving of all respect is confirmed by this man.' The satisfaction Ego feels is noticed by the devoted security guard, Mind, who immediately 'accepts' this person as a friend.

So far so good!

But the next day you discover that this man thinks you are incompetent, or a phony. What happens then?

There's a whole world inside you, parallel to the outside realm, something like the famed wizarding world of Harry Potter, with laws and people and even a mafia operating in there. Ego is now livid at being criticized and his subordinate, Mr Mind, starts to protect the master by instantly 'rejecting' the attacker and dismissing his scathing remarks.

Thus, in a short span of time, Mind has swung to the extremes of acceptance and rejection.

MIND–INTELLIGENCE PARTNERSHIP

Mind could exult to admit the praise-giver or wail to dismiss the critic as an enemy. But it needs help in protecting Ego. He thus draws strength from his dutiful partner, Mr Intelligence.

Intelligence acts swiftly – he provides plans, arguments and 'logical' reasoning to confirm what Mind has accepted or rejected.

In this case, Intelligence says this about your friend on the first day: 'He's got a degree from Harvard and has over 30 years of experience, so naturally, he's right in his views, and he's a loveable person.' The next day, however, after Mind's wailing and disapproval, Intelligence quickly reasons, 'Being from Harvard makes him proud; three decades of experience breeds arrogance. He's senile and should have retired long ago.'

Ego's decree: 'I am the smartest in my office/college/I am the best.'

Mind's reaction to your friend's behaviour: He is 'good' or 'bad'; I 'accept' or 'reject' him.

Intelligence's reason: Logical analysis of why or how he is good or bad; why he should be accepted or rejected.

Then, we have our senses: Our ears, nose, tongue, eyes, and touch. They simply execute the orders of Mind and Intelligence dutifully.

Mind and the Intelligence are friends. Their existence is a fast, intertwined dance and you wouldn't know when these two security guards have leapt to embrace the flatterer or crushed the enemy in a deathly, albeit rhythmic waltz. The duo's presence seems innocuous in our inside world, and little do we realize that we are slaves to these two demons.

FROM 'FALSE' TO 'REAL' EGO

At this point, it is important to differentiate between 'False' and 'Real' Ego.

The internal moods of fear, anger, greed, envy, insecurity – all life-alienating belief systems – reveal that our consciousness has been contaminated, and it is the 'False' Ego in operation here. When a person internalizes the values of service, humility, appreciation – all life-enhancing principles – his 'Real' Ego state has been awakened. Such a person is an evolved being for whom the mind and intelligence act as friends.

Unfortunately, when we live at the level of the False Ego, far from using our mind and intelligence, we are being used by them.

And that's because we have lost our real identity or the Real Ego: the 'I' becomes the contaminated consciousness or the False Ego.

To regain control of our lives, we need to confront the False Ego and show it its true place; it is not the master but a servant.

When your intention is to want to serve others in some way beyond just fulfilling your own needs or, in other words, when you seek to love, practise gratitude, give to others or spread goodness, you have awakened your Real Ego. And this takes many years of practice to correct. But, as later chapters will reveal, even a tiny step in the right direction – small acts of kindness, love, gratitude and so on – help us tap into the real self. Over a period of time, with right actions practised consistently, we move from a 'false' sense of identity to a 'real' one. And that's when the mind has truly become our friend.

While Mind seeks to defend Ego's desires, Intelligence acts as an obedient servant to the mind. A man who kills in the name of his religion may be driven by a False Ego (I am the greatest and my religion is the only path to God) and his mind may then 'accept' and 'reject' people, relationships and activities based on this fundamental order of Ego. Intelligence then plans a massive terror strike on all non-believers, and while the world is stunned by this dastardly deed and you are wondering how any human being could commit such an act, the man in question has no qualms about it. He is convinced that this was the best thing to do because his intelligence justified the monstrous acts as the will of God. As the thirteenth-century Persian poet and Sufi mystic Jalaluddin Rumi said, 'The ego is a veil between humans and God.'

The mindset driven by the False Ego has been revealed in the Bhagavad Gita: 'Bewildered by false ego, strength, pride, lust and anger, the demons become envious of the Supreme Personality of Godhead, who is situated in their own bodies and in the bodies of others, and blaspheme against the real religion' (16.18).

This also answers the question of why we think the way we do and why we hate endlessly or remain confused about our choices.

Our biases, prejudices, likes and dislikes are simply an interplay of this trio in action.

Therefore, let us take a step backwards by questioning our own beliefs and values, rather than judging others. Let us work on reviving the Real Ego, the purified consciousness where the 'I' is an eternal being full of happiness and driven by loving service.

And then you'll be pleasantly surprised to discover that you have two beloved friends in your inner world who can help you to discover inner peace and to spread this happiness all around.

But there is a little more you need to know. I'm referring to the three 'energies' that brainwash or influence the mind. I'll discuss this in Chapter 2.

SUMMARY

- Ego: The unseen boss of the gang, he simply pronounces a decree like, 'I am the greatest' or 'I deserve more than others'. Mind and Intelligence execute the order.
- Mind: As the first servant of Ego, he immediately 'accepts' or 'rejects' people, places, situations based on Ego's diktat.
- Intelligence: Second-in-command, he provides plans, justifications and ideas to 'accept' or 'reject' Ego's desire.
- Senses: They execute the order of Mind and Intelligence through the ears, nose, tongue, eyes and the sense of touch.
- The recipe for a happy life is to transform the 'False' Ego into the 'Real' Ego by cultivating the right kind of foundational attitudes such as: 'I want to serve'; 'I love, not exploit'; or 'I am in gratitude'.
- These purified inner aspirations help us transform our inner 'enemies' into 'friends'.

CHAPTER TWO

The Three Invisible Ropes

'People in this world are tightly bound by the power of my three energies and only one who surrenders to me can overcome it.'

— Bhagavad Gita (7.14)

ONE EVENING, AS I meditated on our ashram's terrace, my neighbour waved to me spiritedly from his balcony. I acknowledged him even as I continued chanting softly. He shouted out that he had seen me chant in the mornings as well, and wondered what it was all about. Eventually, once I was done with my mediation, we began chatting. Soon, we had become friends.

Uday shared his passion for music with me and also inquired about my spiritual practices. He was a connoisseur of good music – he rose early each day and played the soothing 'Call of the Valley' on his Bose speakers. He said that Pandit Shivkumar Sharma's santoor and Pandit Hariprasad Chaurasia's flute transported his soul to a spiritual realm.

Later in the afternoon, his speakers would blast romantic Bollywood songs. After 8 p.m., he played AC/DC's 'Highway to Hell'. He confessed that heavy metal and hard rock helped him vent the animal within him. He'd gulp a few pegs of whisky and swoon in honour of Bon Scott, the lead singer who, within months of recording this song, had died after a night of heavy drinking.

One day, I talked to him about the science of improving self-awareness by recognizing the three invisible 'ropes' or energies that control our lives. He was curious about them and I suggested an experiment that would explain this concept better.

I asked him to play his favourite rock-and-roll or Bollywood songs early in the morning. And, at night, when the 'animal' within him demanded the experience of Robert Plant or Suzi Quatro, he could instead play soft Hindustani classical music. Although amused at my proposal, he was game.

Two days after the musical swap, he confessed it was a miserable experience; he just wasn't getting the same feel.

'What is wrong?' I probed.

'It's just not the same,' he said, unable to explain any further.

I offered him an explanation: 'Could it be that the morning hours are surcharged with an energy that helps us connect to a deeper, spiritual self? If we go for a walk during the predawn hours, we'd likely feel a general sense of well-being. Afternoons, however, are imbued with the vigour of action and passion; and nights carry the force of inertia that helps our bodies rest.'

My friend thought it was a subtle but reasonable explanation. I continued: 'When the potency of Goodness is prominent, one feels peaceful and satisfied. When Passion rules, it's about hurrying; creation and action. And if Ignorance is the overwhelming force, there is inertia and darkness, even destruction and madness.'

Then, I connected these energies to his experience with music, for even music has its own energies and can be experienced in different modes. The sound and melody can soothe, agitate or provoke irrational reactions depending on whether the primary mode or energy of the music is sattva, rajas or tamas. There are three such energies that exist in nature: sattva, Goodness; rajas, Passion; and tamas, Ignorance.

Uday immediately quipped, 'No wonder your temples open so early in the morning, when the bars shut. I guess that's because mornings are conducive for a connection with God and the night is the best time to drown our sorrows in liquor or go off to sleep.'

I nodded as he then recalled how a large number of rock stars had self-destructive habits; the blend of their music and night-time addictions only accentuating their tamas.

THE THREE ENERGIES IN ACTION

Now, let me explain clearly what these three energies or modes are. An hour and a half before sunrise, the mode of Goodness prevails in the atmosphere. This is evidenced by a certain calmness and peace in the air that inspires some to rise early and offer prayers. Most yoga and meditation enthusiasts recommend early morning sessions, as they are most conducive not only for maintaining good physical health but also for inner reflection and spiritual progress.

After the sun has fully risen and up until late evening, the mode of Passion dominates the atmosphere. During this time, people are naturally inclined and inspired to perform activities in the external world: The streets are busy and crowded, people are at work, markets are crowded with shoppers. The rush-hour traffic is a good example of the noise, activity and chaos that characterize this part of the day, reflecting life in the mode of Passion.

The night is conducive for sleep and the recuperation of the body, and this is the mode of Ignorance. Tamas can also be explained through other words such as inertia, lethargy, dullness or darkness. After a hard day's work, the body calms down and rests during this period and the atmosphere facilitates a good break as the mode of Ignorance puts one off to sleep. For a healthy and balanced life, it helps if you retire before 10 p.m. and rise fresh and energetic before 4 a.m.

Today, however, the situation is rather different. People work late hours; their social lives keep them busy till the wee hours. Being influenced by the mode of Ignorance, many even lose their sense of discrimination – they drink too much, indulge in reckless behaviour like rash driving, become prone to anger and other extreme emotions, and so on. The night hours are also the time that crimes are committed – it is not a coincidence that many things are done under the cover of darkness! Meanwhile, nature, through the energy of Ignorance, is clearly instructing us to relax at night.

THE INVISIBLE ROPES

The Bhagavad Gita calls sattva, rajas and tamas 'gunas', which literally means a rope.

For instance, a jockey may restrict the movement of his horse with his reins. Or you can think of the strings from which a puppet dangles. Likewise, these three invisible ropes – sattva, rajas and tamas – bind us to certain qualities, thoughts, feelings and activities. The energy is all-pervading. Everything – all actions, behaviour, thoughts – are influenced by these three modes.

A discerning observer can perceive a park emanating sattva early in the morning, but a few hours later, at the same place, he'll feel rajas as he sees strangers quarrel over a trifle. Later, as crows feast on the piles of open garbage outside the park, the stench and filth inspire tamasic feelings of disgust within him.

Often, the mixing and churning of these energies is instant and dynamic, and one can't quite catch it intellectually – it's too fast for the human mind to grasp. Although it's not easy to recognize the pull and push of the modes, if we can make more sattva choices, we will be able to recognize the influence of the modes on us. For example, if you chose to rise early and practise yoga or meditation, or do some journaling, you have made a sattva choice. This improves clarity of thought and not only keeps you peaceful, but also helps you discern the interplay of the modes in your external and internal surroundings.

That happens because in a sattva state you rise above the rajasic speed and tamasic sleep; you are now more self-aware and thereby have a clear mind. Without this clarity, the mind dominates the awareness and you become muddled with many thoughts and feelings. Without sattva as the default setting of the mind, you are like a puppet pulled by strings – rajas and tamas will quickly drag you down. Sattva immediately helps you raise your energy, moving beyond the influence of Passion and Ignorance.

THE PRE-DAWN ADVANTAGE

What is common to Mahatma Gandhi, Tim Cook, Michelle Obama, Ursula Burns, Jeff Immelt, Indra Nooyi, Narendra Modi and Jack Dorsey?

There's something they all do that many may not be aware of, but it could very well be the silent and steady cause of their success. They rise each morning before 5 a.m.

Does that help?

Imagine a crystal clear lake, tranquil in the morning mist. If you throw a stone right in the middle of it, you will see graceful ripples spreading from the centre; the lake will dance rhythmically in response to that one small stone.

When you wake up early in the morning, the mind's lake is fresh and still. That's when you have a choice – to throw in a thought pebble. The choice of which thought to pick and throw into the mind is entirely yours. But the ripples that follow are beyond your control. You will be a mute spectator to the dance that follows – it could be a thought of positivity or boredom, or worse, negative emotions could engulf your mind.

If you have thrown in a 'stone' of gratitude early in the morning, you'll likely see positive possibilities even later in the day. If you unwittingly drop a pebble of regret or a feeling of inadequacy, you could be moaning all day. And it all begins with that one 'stone' that you chose to drop into the clear lake of your mind.

The morning is God's way of saying that it's a new day, and we can start all over again. It's a chance for us to take birth again, to write a new chapter in the Book of Life!

Since the morning hours are permeated with sattva, when you add conscious positive thoughts to it, you get a synergetic effect that ripples through the rest of the day.

MAKE THE RIGHT CHOICE!

There are many people who prefer waking up late, say at 10 a.m. They can make a sattva choice with consciously chosen positive thoughts. A grateful thought is sattva, even if it's at midnight, and cheating someone is tamas, even if it's early in the morning. When we make a negative choice upon rising from the bed, we have dropped a meaningless 'stone' into the lake. The result is that the mind's ripples drag us helplessly into the same negative thought patterns. This is the tamas of the previous night carried forward the next morning, but with more intensity.

If the first thing you do on waking up is brood over your boss and her temperamental behaviour, or fantasize about revenge (tamas), you invite needless anxiety during your office hours (more tamas). Remember: the first thing we do when we rise sets the ball rolling for the rest of the day.

We want to be happy. We want everything in our lives to settle just the way we like, but little do we realize that we have little or no control on the world and other people. We can, however, make the right choices in our inner world. When our internal sattva choices and the external sattva environment combine, we create a beautiful world both within and without.

Therefore, mornings are the best time for prayers and introspection. And it all begins with the first thought and practice of the day. Steve Jobs revealed in his Stanford address in 2005 that 'for the past 33 years, I have looked in the mirror every morning and asked myself: "If today were the last day of my life, would I want to do what I am about to do today?" And whenever the answer has been "no" for too many days, I know I need to change something.'

During the day, traffic gets busier, cars honk, the air is polluted with smoke and there are far too many people on the roads. But early in the morning, you can drive smoothly on a clear road. Likewise, as the day progresses, the mind gets clogged up with thousands of issues. But early in the morning, you can drive a long distance on your inner journey. There is clarity as the muddle hasn't yet crept in. Before it does, you can choose gratitude and prayers. You'll then be gone a long distance into the realm of divinity – a whole different world of positivity and grace – before the daily business settles in. By the time the distracting, negative elements ready themselves to strike within your mind, you'll already be a safe distance away from them.

A habit of being in the 'present' early in the morning helps you practise mindfulness for the rest of the day. Many spiritualists spend their precious predawn hours chanting, praying and meditating. They are then equipped to face the day's myriad challenges.

Many of our emotional problems can be cured through these simple methods. It's regrettable if we waste our precious morning hours on sleep, Facebook updates or the news. Social media activity simply captures the mind and compels us to react to external influences. Somebody else and something else invades our consciousness. You've let someone else throw pebbles into the lake of your mind!

Richard Whatley, a nineteenth-century English theologian and a prolific writer, nailed it when he said, 'Lose an hour in the morning and you will spend all day looking for it.' Whatley was paralysed on his left side during his later years. Yet, he continued his public duties and his fruitful writing. His morning habits helped him do this.

If we want to be happy, we need to rise above the influence of the modes on our minds. And that means we need to first recognize our real self as different from this body, and then care for the self's needs.

TAKING CARE OF THE REAL SELF:
THE BODY vs. THE SOUL

Socrates, the greatest thinker of his time, was convicted of corrupting the young minds of Athens. His death sentence was to drink the deadly hemlock.

His disciple, Crito, told him how he could escape prison. Some of his followers also bribed the guards. But Socrates refused to leave. He believed the act would indicate a fear of death, when he actually wasn't afraid. When the guards threatened to kill him, he calmly replied, 'First, you need to find me, then you can consider killing me.' The response confused the guards. What Socrates had referred to was his soul. He knew his body could be destroyed by soldiers at any moment, but he was not that temporary garment – the body – that is abandoned in time by the soul to obtain another one.

After taking the poison, Socrates was ordered to walk around until his legs felt numb. Soon, he collapsed. Moments before his death, Socrates spoke his last words to Crito: 'We owe a gift to Asclepius; Crito, please don't forget to pay the debt.'

Asclepius was the Greek god for curing illness and Socrates's last words meant that Asclepius had cured him of the biggest disease – the body. By granting him death, the god had freed his soul from all suffering.

When someone asks us about our identity, we spontaneously declare 'I am Ramesh' or 'I am the senior manager' or 'I am a mother of two children' or 'I am a Gujarati'. Little do we realize that our state of being – the real 'I' – is eternal; it's beyond all these temporary states.

Your name, designation, religion, gender, marital status can all change, yet there is something about you that won't change at all. You may not remember anything you did as a five-year-old, and the chemical makeup within you has changed since then; yet, you are still the same person. The body ages and deteriorates, but there is an eternity within you that time cannot destroy.

Once we recognize that we have an existence separate from our bodies, our spiritual journey begins.

The Vedic texts, especially the Bhagavad Gita (the second chapter), explains that we are essentially a pure spirit soul that is eternal in nature and we have an existence separate from our present bodies. Yet, the soul, trapped within this temporary body, now manoeuvres it in the same way a driver manipulates his car on the road.

A car needs petrol as energy, but the driver's fuel is different. Likewise, we may exercise or eat or dress nicely, but the real self – the spirit soul – that resides within this car-like body needs a different kind of nourishment. Only when we can satisfy the needs of the soul do we find lasting contentment.

One may polish the golden cage but starve the bird within. In the same manner, many people are unable to nourish their souls due to an overwhelming absorption in bodily issues. To compound their misery, the three modes of nature disconnect them further from their real self.

What are the real needs of the soul, and how do we fulfil them even as the modes pull us in different directions?

To recognize the soul's needs, we need to first situate ourselves in sattva. It's in Goodness that you hear a voice over and above the mind's noise. Sattva methods also help us recognize how the three modes cover our souls – as revealed in the exercise below.

I learnt this game from a friend, which explains the three modes effectively.

Three volunteers come forward to face the audience. They choose from three pairs of gloves: one of them puts on a surgeon's gloves, the second a cricket player's, and the third a pair of boxer's gloves. Then, they are each handed a thread and a needle. The challenge is to pass the thread through the eye of the needle in three minutes.

As the countdown begins, each one of them scrambles to get it done within the time limit. Needless to say, the person wearing the surgeon's gloves is the first to pass the thread. The one with the cricketer's gloves takes a little longer, and the boxer is a non-starter. He's hardly able to even hold the thread and the needle, and has certainly lost the game from the word go. As the audience laughs at the clumsiness of the cricketer and the boxer, it's obvious to all that what's natural and easy to do with a free hand is difficult and artificial when it's covered with gloves.

After the game, we ask the audience what they learnt from the exercise. Most get the point – the free hand represents the uncovered, pure spirit soul and the three different gloves represent the three modes. The surgeon's gloves denote the mode of Goodness, the cricketer's stands for Passion and the boxer's gloves indicate Ignorance. To the degree that the hand is covered, it is difficult to thread the needle. Likewise, to the extent that the soul is covered, our activities and freedom are concealed.

Just as a surgeon's gloves are quite fine and comfortable, and caused the least inconvenience in threading the needle, the mode of Goodness, although it is a covering on the soul, nevertheless provides more freedom and facility to act. Feeling an inner contentment, a person in the mode of Goodness finds life comfortable and happy.

Since the cricketer's gloves are thicker than that of the surgeon's, there's more difficulty in pulling the thread through the eye of the needle. In parallel, the mode of Passion as compared to Goodness provides lesser freedom to act, and causes an inherent dissatisfaction and agitation in the consciousness of a person. And the mode of Ignorance totally covers up the identity and the spiritual nature of the soul, just as the boxer's gloves completely covered the original shape of the hand. Think of those addicted to drugs, who just can't pull themselves up to make life-enhancing choices. They helplessly submit to tamas.

The modes bind us day in and day out. But if we do make the right sattva choices, we allow sattva to control us; it is a cyclical feed.

An Indian folktale says it best:

Three brothers, Sattva, Rajas and Tamo, walked daily from their village to sell hats in the city. One morning, Tamo left to make his sale and, after a tiring walk, rested under a tree. When he woke up, he saw that all his hats were gone; the monkeys on the branches of the tree had taken them. He was immediately filled with worry and sadness.

'Oh, how will I get money now? I am finished. Life is so harsh and fate so terrible,' moaned Tamo as he walked up to a country bar and got himself drunk to forget his fears.

A little later, Rajas left and, also rested under that tree. Once again, the monkeys took all his hats from the bag. On waking up, Rajas was mad with anger. He hurled the choicest of curses and threw stones at the monkeys, but to no avail. Finally, tired, he left dejected and determined to take revenge on the monkeys.

Sattva left for the city a little later in the day and rested under the same tree. The monkeys took his hats as well. When Sattva woke up and realized what the monkeys had done, he didn't panic or react hastily. He thought for a moment and drew out his own hat from his pocket. Pointing it to the monkeys, he provoked them by repeatedly grinning and frowning. Having captured their attention, he suddenly threw his own hat to the ground. The monkeys followed suit; they threw from the branches all the hats they had gathered. Sattva immediately picked them up and put them back in his bag. Then, quietly and speedily, he left the place. He went to the city, made a good sale, returned home early that evening and rested peacefully at night.

Each of the brothers had the same stimulus, yet they chose to respond differently. Being bound tightly by the mode of Ignorance, Tamo had little choice. He felt helpless and, by making further wrong choices, he only aggravated his misery. Rajas, being bound up by the mode of Passion, couldn't help himself either. Sattva could think and act clearly because the modes had the least binding effect on him; he was situated primarily in the mode of Goodness.

The purity and wisdom of sattva helps us think clearly while those in the mode of Passion are driven to anger. The purity and wisdom of sattva helps us think clearly while those in the mode of Passion are driven to anger; they can also be hungry for wealth and fame. Those trapped by the mode of Ignorance are lazy, addicted to intoxicants and always miserable.

SIMPLE 'CHOICE' PRACTICES

When one takes drugs for the first time, he allows tamas to bind him. The next time he's offered drugs, in order to say 'no' and thus choose rightly he has to wage a *war* against tamas. If he succumbs to the drugs, then his ability to make the right choices is further weakened. He's thus trapped in a vicious cycle. This is why many addicts feel helpless, and consider any methods of help such as support groups and 'self-help talk' rubbish. They have been abused by their minds and victimized by tamas. For many, this inner turmoil reflects in failed relationships. Their inability to get people to love them is due to their own lack of self-love.

Alternatively, there is a virtuous cycle in nature too. If you choose to rise early and spend time with nature, the experience of sattva will nourish you. Somewhere, this healthy deposit of good practises strengthens your desire to seek sattva again. Daily, unlimited choices confront us and the more we choose sattva, the more likely we are to be in control of our lives. Alternatively, if we send hate mail or indulge in unkind talk about others, or choose to smoke and drink, the more we lose control over and balance in our lives.

Like gravity pulls things downwards in this world, the lower modes – especially tamas – pull us down all the time. If you seek sattva (say you want to be kind and generous), which is like defying gravity, don't be surprised if rajas demands attention. And if you are predominantly leading a rajas lifestyle, busy and restless, then tamas (drugs, liquor or violence) could threaten to drag you down.

The good news is that we can choose to break free from the lower modes. By consciously cultivating thoughts and activities in the higher mode, we can break the habits and patterns cultivated in the mode of Ignorance. As each energy tries to dominate your mind, it's imperative to add ample sattva choices to your life such as rising early, exercise, prayer, meditation and writing in your journal. The coming chapters in the book discuss how we can add more sattva in our lives.

All the little things we do daily add to the pattern of a particular mode or a combination of modes. This then shapes our personality and behaviour; we have thus determined the influence of these modes on ourselves.

THE DIFFERENT DEGREES OF HAPPINESS IN THE THREE MODES

By now, you would have understood clearly the difference in the three energies, and how and when they operate in our lives.

The Bhagavad Gita succinctly describes happiness in the three modes:

'That which in the beginning may be just like poison but at the end is just like nectar and which awakens one to self-realization is said to be happiness in the mode of goodness. That happiness which is derived from contact of the senses with their objects and which appears like nectar at first but poison at the end is said to be of the nature of passion. And that happiness which is blind to self-realization, which is delusion from beginning to end and which arises from sleep, laziness and illusion is said to be of the nature of ignorance.' (18.37–39)

Basically, long-term happiness or a feeling of lasting contentment is in the mode of Goodness; short-term pleasure that ends in guilt or pain is in the mode of passion; and destructive thoughts and activities, where one only imagines some form of pleasure, is in the mode of Ignorance. All kinds of intoxicants fall into this category.

Food, music, and even the clothes you wear are influenced by the modes.

Foods like fresh fruits, vegetables, grains, nuts and non-violent milk products, which improve the quality of one's life and are eaten in moderate quantities, are examples of food in the mode of Goodness.

The mode of Passion in food has extreme taste and is eaten in excess. Such food causes pain and misery. It is said that passionate food burns when it goes in, and also when it comes out! The happiness derived from such food is only tongue-deep and short-lived. Such foods create disease in the body and compromise on the quality of our lives.

Animal fat and meat products that result from violence and the slaughter of animals are highly tamas. All kinds of intoxicants and drugs also degrade the self and are in the mode of Ignorance.

Music can, for example, inspire serenity, or evoke lust or even agitate you to craziness. My friend Uday shared this story:

'A reporter from a prestigious English newspaper was touring the remote villages of Bihar. She was astonished to see a lone farmer lying on a cot in a small wheat field, while hard-rock music blasted out from a loudspeaker nearby. She wondered what drew the rustic farmer, who seemed so alien to the Western ways of life, to this music; it certainly appeared incongruent. She asked him with a blend of surprise and amusement how he had developed a taste for this sound. "I don't know what the hell this is," answered the farmer sleepily, "but since I began playing this music, none of the jackals or crows dare to come to my field."'

If you take a bath and wear fresh clothes, you have opted for sattva. If you wear tight clothes that are flashy and provoke sensuality in you and others, then they carry the energy of rajas. And your stonewashed blue jeans that have been unwashed for weeks carry latent tamas because it's dirty.

WHERE ARE WE HEADING?

We are not bound by a single mode. The three modes affect us like a rope. To make a rope, you twist fibre in a threefold process: First, it is twisted into three small strands. Then, the three are once again twisted together, and finally those three strands are bound as one. This way the rope becomes strong.

Likewise, the three modes are mixed in us right from our birth, and they keep combining again and again from then on. The modes are mixed again and again because we often live without awareness or conscious choices of what enters our mind. Consequently, for an ordinary person whose inner life is unregulated, the modes are 'twisted together' innumerable times.

Sattva is a platform to ensure not only a peaceful and aware mind living in the present but also to help us to make a better future. It is the 'now' that helps us eliminate our past mistakes. Today, we can rewrite our future physical and mental well-being. To paraphrase a famous quote I once heard: What happens to us does not have to define who we are, and my past cannot control my future unless I allow it to.

What are the simple ways to live in sattva? Chapter 3 will offer a simple but often-ignored tool.

SUMMARY

- The three energies or modes that exist all around us are: Goodness (sattva), Passion (rajas) and Ignorance (tamas).
- People behave differently in the same situation because of the influence of the three modes.
- The influence of the three modes of nature:

Three modes	Food	Music	Time of the day
Goodness	Fresh fruits, vegetables, and grains	Soft; inspires serenity and peace	An hour-and-a-half before sunrise
Passion	Hot and burning foods	Loud; increases desires	Sunrise to sunset
Ignorance	Meat, intoxicants and drugs	Provocative, loud, lewd or negative lyrics; intoxication is a common feature	Night

- We can use the three modes to our advantage by rising early, like most successful people of this world. Healthy activity during predawn hours is like dropping a pebble into a crystal-clear lake – it creates beautiful ripples in the lake of the mind for the rest of the day.
- Our first choice of a mode immediately binds us and provokes further choices and their consequences. For example: The first sample of drugs makes it easier to do drugs again and a habit is formed easily.
- Little sattva choices done daily can help us improve our awareness and thereby gain more control on our inner lives.

CHAPTER THREE

Observe More, Judge Less

'Yet in this body resides another, one who observes and permits – he's known as the Supersoul.'
— Bhagavad Gita (13.23)

I WAS ON A flight once and saw a passenger stand up from his seat. His eyes were red and his forehead was wet with perspiration. He looked around, his face twitching, and then with a sudden grin, he hurriedly sat down again. A few seconds later, he rose again and paced up and down the aisle, murmuring to himself. The lady who sat next to him was reading a book, but occasionally she would look at him, her lips curled in an expressionless countenance.

He's definitely angry with his wife, I thought to myself. Then I instantly realized I'd made a judgement. I told myself not to make any judgements but to just observe. Why was my judgement problematic? Firstly, how could I say with any certainty that the man was angry? And how did I know she was his wife? Perhaps I was right in my guesses, but my conclusions were speculations at best.

AN HONEST SCIENTIST

Judgements, even without our awareness, often follow our observations.

Ideally, if we are scientific in our approach, we make a hypothesis, conduct experiments, observe and only then draw conclusions. But many of us judge too quickly. When we see things, people, behaviours and events that confirm our beliefs, we draw strong judgements. Life goes on with more theories, observations and judgements; but we are averse to the truth because we are convinced we are right. As someone once said, 'My mind is made up; don't confuse me with the facts.'

If you say Rohit Sharma is a great batsman, that's a judgement, albeit a good one. But, here again, my 'good' declaration is also a judgement. Alternatively, if you said Rohit scored three centuries, including a double century, in as many matches, you have simply observed. To say someone is characterless is a ruling, but you could as well say that he sent four e-mails in a single day disowning his family, which would just be an observation of facts.

I can hear you say: *But I am expected to judge to decide better in life!* Maybe you wish you had a stronger sense of discrimination and more clarity in your thought and decisions?

As ironical as it may sound, to improve judgement, we need to give up judgement.

When you observe without attaching labels, you release yourself from your disarrayed mind and enter a higher dimension of reality. This is a platform beyond your own biases and prejudices. Often, we err because we observe little and doubt a lot. Instead, if we observe more and analyse less, it is likely we'll see the real picture.

Observation practises are like bright sunshine; they help us remove the fog of confusion and drive forward, safe and fast. As Rumi said, 'Everyone sees the unseen in proportion to the clarity of their heart.'

Unfortunately, when it comes to our lives, many of us aren't honest scientists. We carry unshakable opinions of ourselves and others. We think we know who we are and we are also convinced that our prejudices are correct. But the sad truth is, somewhere, we've lost the connection to our own self and this world.

PRACTISING OBSERVATION

Once, while riding in an Uber, I found myself deeply stressed. I had spent the last two days in intense meetings, which had produced strong reactions in me. I was feeling judgemental and I was seething with anger, upset with some members of the ashram. I strongly disapproved of the decisions that had been taken and was feeling mentally clogged. I needed a break!

Just then, I felt inspired to see the city from my cab window. I decided to stop my judgements and only observe for the next 10 minutes. I began the inner ride even as the taxi honked and sped through the Mumbai traffic.

I saw a couple speed furiously on a bike, honking and swerving dangerously on the busy road, keeping pace with my cab. Instantly, I judged the young man driving the bike as irresponsible and crazy, and I feared for their safety. Then, my thoughts raced through many subjects: A distant relative who had died in a motorbike crash years ago, my academic achievements, my lovely parents, envious friends and even my cousin's marble-stone business.

Wait, I told myself. This was my moment of clarity: I saw that instead of observing the road, my thoughts had gone all over the place. I instinctively admonished myself for losing five precious minutes recklessly imagining scenarios that had no bearing on my present.

But I had been fooled by the mind again. It had entered through the back door and my feeling inadequate at my mind's terrible wandering was yet another trick!

The way out of this messy entanglement was simple. I said to myself, Come back, dear mind, and observe without judging.

I returned to looking outside the window. I saw a construction site with many workers labouring away; there were shops and temples crowded with men and women dressed in colourful attire. I saw children returning from school and cricket matches being played in narrow by-lanes. Occasionally, I would judge these events or wander off into the past or to the future, but as I gently brought my mind back to the present, I entered the 'awareness' space, because I could now easily catch my wandering mind. If you are thinking all the time, you lose the present and fall back to either the past or jump ahead to the future.

This daily practise of 'observation' over the last three years has helped me handle disputes and heated meetings more effectively. I can check my judgements more often and my close friends have also appreciated my transformation over the years.

Going back to the example in the plane, I saw the man pacing 'angrily' and his 'disinterested' 'wife' sitting next to him, but when I saw myself judging him as 'angry', I had successfully 'observed' myself.

Now, say you were that man striding back and forth in the aisle of the plane and imagine for a moment that you had divine powers through which you could stand away from yourself. Wouldn't it then be an exciting experience to witness your anger, restlessness and other emotions? Even occasionally, if we could 'see' ourselves, we'd immediately be able to bring our lives back on track. That's because you now have an aerial view of your life. It's like watching your house from a helicopter above – you can get a better view from up there than when you are inside the house. Likewise, if you always live inside your head, it helps once in a while to rise above it and get an aerial view of your life.

Regrettably, many of us are not scientists. We neither have the patience to make unbiased observations nor the humility to check our theories. We also lack the courage to abandon our beliefs if we find evidence contrary to our ideas. Instead, we're likely resort to confirmation bias – seeking evidence that justifies *our* preconceptions.

The first step, therefore, is to become an honest spiritual scientist, one who decides to embark on an inner journey by first observing his or her own life. There are examples of scientists who have overlooked evidences contrary to their theories and held on to their own flawed assumptions. Similarly, we might have made conclusions about so many things without an honest approach.

HOW DOES OBSERVATION HELP?

Once, during my travels to different monasteries, I shared a room with a colleague who wouldn't usually carry his keys when he stepped outside. The room had a self-locking door. Often, he'd be inconvenienced on his return if I wasn't inside. I casually mentioned this to a young monk who assisted us.

One day, I was scheduled to travel far and return later at night. My colleague had already left the room and was at the temple doing his prayer practises. Meanwhile, my young assistant, who was to accompany me on my journey, realized that if my friend didn't have his keys he'd be stranded outside for a long time. In a split second, he ran to the temple, gave him the keys and joined me on my travel.

Since I had been practising 'observe, don't judge' exercises, I had noticed this young man offer various services to us. Later in the day, when we were travelling back to the monastery, we casually spoke about different things, including his marriage the next month. I spontaneously recalled how during the early hours he had shown remarkable presence of mind. I appreciated his alertness in his services, but he dismissed it as a small thing. I assured him that this was critical help he had offered. Amid our lighthearted conversation, I commented that his fiancée was very fortunate to have a husband like him. He blushed and our happy exchanges helped us enter a life-enhancing space of appreciation and kindness.

Unknowingly, that evening, I had practised a valuable life principle: Catch them doing right. We often catch people doing wrong, but if we could see and appreciate the nice things happening around us, we'd spread a lot of love. During that journey I had done exactly that. I spoke little that day, but contributed more because I was observing rather than judging. The founder of the Scouts movement, Robert Baden Powell, put it brilliantly: 'If you make listening and observation your occupation, you will gain much more than you can by talking.'

When I look back, there have been many occasions in life when I was busy and so absorbed in my daily activities and in myself that I failed to observe the goodness around me. When our lives are embedded in our own mental world, we become the proverbial frog in the well; we are unable to appreciate the ocean of goodness that thrives outside of our tiny selfish existence. Unfortunately, we rely too much on our powers of reasoning and pretend we understand the world because we use our intellect. Little do we realize that our brain can comprehend only a part of the truth. But, when we choose to practise non-judgemental observation, we go deeper into our selves, and can easily catch the grace around us.

It's only when we choose to listen, to observe, that we journey from our heads to our heart. That's when we access wisdom that's inherent to us.

Chapter 4 reveals, through a case study, the principle at play when we observe living in the present moment.

SUMMARY

- Most of the time, even without your awareness, your judgements follow your observations.
- A paradox: To improve your judgement, you need to practise more observation and negate any judgement.
- Fifteen minutes of observation without judgement will help you improve awareness and connect you to your inner world of values and beliefs.
- During observation, if you catch yourself judging, gently release the thought and draw yourself back to being an observer.
- Over a period of time, this practise will help to connect with the good things around you, which have lain unnoticed so far. This in turn will improve your ability to judge.

A Space beyond the Mind

*'Lord Krishna said: O mighty armed son of Kunti, it is
undoubtedly very difficult to curb the restless mind, but it is
possible by suitable practice and detachment.'*
— Bhagavad Gita (6.35)

THE CRICKETER RAHUL DRAVID was down and out, almost. He
came in to bat at number six in the second innings, in the follow-
on of a match that India was quickly losing. As he prepared to
face the ball, the Australian captain made a scathing remark, 'Oh,
Rahul, is number six now; next match, he'll be number twelve.'
He meant that Rahul was playing so badly that he'd be out of the
team soon. This was a sharp comment to discourage a player who
was already going through a lean phase and was on the verge of
being ousted from the team.

Rahul had seen a bout of low scores in the past, and, even
in this series against the Aussies, he and the Indian team had
fared miserably. He felt shaken as he prepared to bat. He was
now intimidated by his aggressive opponents, who were among
the best in the art of sledging – a ploy to distract a batsman and
disturb his concentration with sarcastic insults, which could cause
him to make mistakes and get dismissed.

What did Rahul do? He decided to take it one ball at a time.
He told himself there was nothing he could do about the past and

he had no control over his fate after this match. But this innings was his. And, to be more precise, the ball that was coming at him was the only reality of his life. *This ball is mine and I will play it to perfection*, he told himself. Meanwhile the Aussies tried their best to see the back of him, but Rahul Dravid stood tall at the crease, living one ball at a time.

What happened then is an incredible story of grit. Along with his partner, V.V.S. Laxman, Rahul batted through the entire fourth day and, most astonishingly, the Indian team came back to life, turned the aggressor and won a match that is widely considered to be one of the greatest matches in Test cricket history. Rahul Dravid had carved his name in cricket folklore, and he made it happen because he did what the American philosopher Henry David Thoreau said: 'The meeting of two eternities – past and future – is precisely the present moment.'

It's absolutely vital for our well-being to live in the present. That doesn't mean we don't plan our future or analyse our past mistakes. It simply means that when you are eating, just eat; and when you are studying, just study. When you plan, do it mindfully. Don't mix up many activities or multitask and end up mentally exhausted. Play one ball at a time!

The mind can offer many scripts and each appears very convincing. If you ignore one proposal of the mind, it presents one more, and then another one, until you succumb. Like this, we remain dutiful slaves to the mind. In the process, we miss out on a simple, yet most effective tool to puncture the mind's tirade. And that is to simply be present in the here and now. The real force and power in this world is always in the now.

In the spiritual tradition I come from, we softly chant the holy names of God on our prayer beads, and the entire focus is on hearing the sound. Bhaktivedanta Swami, who is a revered Bhakti yoga teacher, and the founder of the our global spiritual organization, ISKCON, presented a simple tool: 'Listen to the mantra you are chanting now; there's no question of mind.' He'd say, 'Simply listen.' In other traditions, the details may vary but wherever the practise is to listen or observe or be present, we enter a space beyond the mind; it is here that we touch divinity.

◐◑

Once, I was searching for my umbrella, which I had misplaced. I thought hard and long, but was clueless where I'd last seen it. I gave up, and went about doing other things. Later, as I relaxed, I suddenly knew where I had kept it the previous evening. Sometimes, thinking too hard doesn't work ; we need to relax and keep our thinking aside, and the answer rises up in us.

During one of our monastery meetings, a vexing issue left me clueless and the decision of our ashram authorities disturbed me further. I humbly confessed to my mentor that I was unable to share the same perspective. He suggested I spend the next few days chanting, eating and praying silently, and stop worrying about this incident. In just three days, the whole situation became clear to me and it was as if some incredible realization had occurred in me. Now, everything about the decision made sense to me.

Often, when we try to solve a problem, our mind conjures up many alternatives. But if we slow down and learn to relax, accepting the present in a detached fashion, we'll be surprised by the clarity we receive, even in the midst of great confusion. Many writers, musicians and scientists think hard and for long, yet the 'revelation' happens later, when they aren't consciously thinking about the problem. Mary Shelley, Paul McCartney, Srinivasa Ramanujan, Neils Bohr and Albert Einstein, besides many others, have confessed to accessing areas higher than their conscious awareness when they relaxed or stared at the vast space or simply did nothing.

We deliver our best when we are not trapped by the shackles of the mind; rather, it's the mental freedom that helps us fly and attain great heights. Imagine a cow tied to a pole in a vast farmland. How much area does she have to graze? Likewise, compulsive thinking could inhibit us. But if we learn through these small steps to be in the present, then we can connect to our real potential.

For most people, their potential is inhibited by the mind. When we rise beyond the mind, as Rahul Dravid did in that historic match, we blossom into who we truly are.

When I stay present in conversations, it can help improve my relationships. But I may need an additional tool to help understand others better and also convey my feelings to them. Chapter 5 shares an interesting method to help us do this.

SUMMARY

- Instead of multi-tasking, which leads to mental exhaustion, one should play one ball at a time – when eating, just eat; and when studying, just study.
- The mind's scripts are unlimited and, therefore, the only way out is to be mindful in your present activity.
- When you practise observing, listening, or being present, you enter a space beyond the mind.
- Compulsive thinking can make you more confused; instead, if you relax and accept the present in a detached manner, you will discover solutions from a realm beyond your conscious awareness.

CHAPTER FIVE

Know Your Needs and Feelings

'The mind is restless, turbulent, obstinate and very strong,
O Krishna, and to subdue it, I think, is more difficult than
controlling the wind.'

— Bhagavad Gita (6.34)

RAJESH WAS IN GREAT pain as he talked to me. The abuse and trauma that he had suffered in his past still haunted him. I tried my best to understand him, but he was saying a lot and talking very fast. He spoke about the strong emotions he felt for his family, enemies and colleagues.

Meanwhile, I had had a hectic schedule for about three weeks and badly needed rest. I felt starved of care and empathy myself. I knew a hungry man can't feed others for long. At the same time, I didn't have the heart to interrupt him. Caught in a quandary, I silently prayed for help.

BALANCE COURAGE WITH CONSIDERATION

Do you feel like a victim even as you try to help others? Sometimes people download their worries on you and, despite your sincere desire to serve them, they do not seem to get the benefit of your assistance. On the contrary, they behave badly with you and feel offended if you don't hear them out. You get caught in a vicious cycle as your genuine service, instead of nourishing you, leaves you exhausted. And if you avoid the person he could take you on a guilt trip saying, for example, that he had trusted you to help him and you'd let him down.

But there is hope if, even as you show concern for others, you also display the same compassion for yourself. This requires courage – to take care of the self. And when you do that, you can serve others better.

To return to my stressful session with Rajesh, what happened was that my prayers were answered and soon, I had the calm and clarity I needed. What I did as I sat with him was to breathe mindfully – I heard the breath that I inhaled and slowly exhaled even though, externally, I held Rajesh's hand and continued to listen to him. Inadvertently, as I focused on my breathing, I entered a space beyond my thoughts. I also felt a sense of control over my emotional state. I knew I needed to offer service and add value to others' lives, and this was my chance to do so. I abruptly said, 'I want to understand you, but I am lost. Can you please help me realize what you are going through?'

He stopped talking and stared blankly at me; my request had confused him. Then he nodded as if to accede to my wish. I pulled out of my bag a 'Needs–Feelings' card that Premnidhi dasa, a friend of mine, had given me years ago. I usually carry this card in my bag; it has a list of emotional 'needs' and 'feelings' written on it. This list is based on the principle of Non-Violent Communication developed by Marshall Rosenberg. The card often helps me connect to my own internal state.

I asked the troubled Rajesh to recognize the words that accurately described what he was feeling. He glanced at the sheet once and then continued complaining. My mind protested because I was now aware that Rajesh was treating me like a dustbin. I tried to feel compassion, but it was more practical to stop him and ask him to improve his awareness.

'No,' I said assertively. 'I insist you see the list here and I am sure some words here resonate with your situation now.

I wouldn't want to guess or judge what you are going through. So please help me.'

He said 'okay', but after a few seconds of looking at the list he went off on a tangent again. I banged the table and got up with a start. I summoned all my sincerity and begged him, 'Please help me; I want to serve you, but I feel miserable because I can't.'

He sputtered. 'Let me tell you this one thing, and then I'll listen to you.'

A few minutes passed, and there was no sign he'd stop. I rose again, folded my palms, and said, 'Before we met, you were helpless; now it's two of us who are frustrated. I am sorry; I need to leave now as I feel irritated because I am unable to connect to you.'

'Oh, sorry,' he said. 'You tell me, what should I do?'

CONNECT TO YOUR FEELINGS AND NEEDS TO INCREASE AWARENESS

I pointed to the card on the table and asked him to see it. We shared a few moments of silence; he settled down and stared intently at the feelings mentioned on the card. Then, he pointed to more than 10 feelings. After he finished, I suggested we tackle one feeling at a time and he picked 'Loneliness.' I explained to him that our feelings are a result of certain needs that have been met, and other needs that haven't been fulfilled. I then turned the card and pointed to the 'needs' side and asked him which of his needs were unfulfilled. The words seemed to make a lot of sense to him now; again, he pointed to many needs, and it appeared that we'd again get lost in the forest of his mind.

'You feel lonely because you need…what?' I probed.

After some time, his eyes still on the card, he said, 'Respect – to be heard is my biggest need now.'

I nodded. Slowly, he began to calm down, and the relief on his face spoke a thousand words. He had just experienced awareness. To 'feel' lonely is different from 'knowing' that you are lonely or need respect. Some people are irritable because they are not respected but, unfortunately, they don't know what's annoying them. And if you know you need respect, there is a better chance you'll meet that need and consequently feel less irritated or lonely.

Awareness, therefore, helps us take proper action.

I then advised Rajesh that if he wrote down an action plan that would help him meet his needs, he would be able to move forward happily in his life's journey.

He thanked me as he left and, strangely, I felt thrilled. I looked at the card and realized I was ecstatic because I had just fulfilled my need to make a difference and contribute to the world. But then, I had another pressing need – rest and peace – and Rajesh's positive response ensured rest for me that evening.

Rajesh's case study and the use of the Needs–Feelings card reveal the power of pressing the pause button in the middle of the mind's relentless attack on the self. Chapters 6 to 8 will teach you how to pause, and what to do when you pause.

SUMMARY

- A card containing words that describe your different feelings and needs will help you improve your self-awareness.
- You need to identify your feelings at any given point in time, and check in with the needs you have that have not been met.
- When you know your feelings and needs, you are empowered to recognize your emotional state; to know you are lonely will feel different from being lonely.
- Improved awareness increases the chance of meeting your needs.

CHAPTER SIX

Slow Down to Speed Up

'What is night for all beings is the time of awakening for the self-controlled; and the time of awakening for all beings is night for the introspective sage.'

– Bhagavad Gita (2.69)

IN OUR TEMPLE KIRTANS, just at the climax, the singer pauses for a second. The accompanying cymbals and drums freeze as well. Then, an explosion of sound takes place – the song suddenly reaches a crescendo, and at this point, in perfect sync with the melody, the other instruments are also played. The effect on the participants is tumultuous – they leap up as though in a spiritual frenzy.

This is what actually happens if you just 'pause' during your daily non-stop 'music and dance'.

Studies have shown that for long-term success, one needs to periodically take a break, relax the body and mind, and only then resume one's pursuits. When you consciously slow down, you rejuvenate your bodily and mental muscles.

Just take a look at a sunrise or sunset. Is it sudden or is there a natural pace to it? Things happen organically in nature, following their own rhythm. You can't rush nature; you can't tell a tree to hurry up and grow. However, in our modern world, when we want light, we just have to flip a switch and, in a sudden flash, we experience light. You may marvel at human expertise and progress, but on deeper introspection, you will realize we live an artificial and fast-paced life that is simply not aligned with nature.

The science of yoga teaches one to relax while performing various poses, bending and twisting. Likewise, the science of happy living calls for pressing the pause button as you bend and twist in life.

HOW DO WE PAUSE?

You simply have to relax, and you do that by doing nothing!

Our daily appointments and goals can make our inner world rigid and boring. Further, we spend so much time inside our 'heads' – analysing, worrying, planning, and so on – that we hardly have time for our 'heart'. But the seat of emotions is the heart; that's where inspiration comes from, and purpose flourishes. It's in the heart that ambition meets conscience and where love takes precedence over achievements. Busy with the business of daily living, we often neglect the heart, and the results are disastrous.

A mistake many commit on their frenzied journey through life is to opt for instant self-gratification. Liquor, drugs and sex may seem to bring relief, but the hormone dopamine, released by the brain during such short-term pleasures, soon wears off. Immediately afterwards, another hormone, prolactin, is released, and that causes the exact opposite effect – that of irritability and depression. The result is a cycle of dependence on these hormones.

This volatile fluctuation of neurochemicals in the body weakens the immune system. Diseases strike at the slightest provocation, the body ages faster and your health is severely impacted. The best way to get out of this vicious cycle is to *pause* and improve your self-awareness.

HOW TO IMPROVE SELF-AWARENESS

Conscious Breathing

We all breathe, but are we conscious of it?

In my seminars, I often ask participants to place their hands on their stomachs and feel it as they inhale and exhale. When you breathe in, does your stomach move outwards or inwards? What happens when you exhale? The class is often divided, with half the students claiming that their stomach moves inward during a deep inhale and the other half saying they are unsure. The point driven home is emphatic: We don't even know how to breathe, something which even animals do so naturally. Our disconnect with the self is acute; we need to first learn to breathe normally and *consciously*!

A simple technique is to inhale deeply to the count of four, hold the breath to the count of eight and then exhale slowly to the count of eight. Focus on the sound of your breath; listen carefully as you inhale and exhale. In no time, you'll catch your mind wandering. Gently bring it back to your breathing, and in three to five minutes you'll be recharged with fresh energy.

In case you're wondering if it's practical to relax daily – given your hectic schedule and tight deadlines – ask yourself a simple question: Can I afford to ignore it? What are the long-term costs involved in going against nature?

Time with Nature

If you want fresh air and positive energy, sit under a tree or, better still, hug one.

In his 2005 best-selling book, *Last Child in the Woods*, Richard Louv, a journalist and author of several books on nature, coined the term 'Nature-deficit-disorder'. In the book, he argues that modern humans have become disconnected from nature, and this has negative consequences on physical and mental health.

Back in the 1850s, Henry David Thoreau had written *Walden*, his reflections of the time he spent living alone in a forest for two years. It is considered one of America's most celebrated works of literature. The wisdom of the book is simple: Thoreau exposes the existing materialist and consumerist culture as dangerous, and offers a happy alternative of living simply. He encourages readers to be 'alert' and get in touch with the truths and mysteries in the external world and in the world within. The only way to do this, he says, is by connecting with the self rather than seeking pleasures in an extravagant lifestyle and carnal pursuits. The message rings true even today, 160 years after the book was written.

I like to remember what Steven Covey, one of the most influential management gurus of the twentieth century, called the 'Law of the Farm', where things happen slowly and organically. You plant the seeds, wait for the rain, then harvest them, and eventually get the produce at the right time. But we are used to quick results. He calls it the 'Law of Exam', where we study at the last minute, cram the answers and forget them immediately after we reproduce them on the answer sheet.

Instant gratification is the norm today, and slow and introspective living is almost frowned upon. It's likely that if you admit your inability to attend a social function because of some office deadline, you'll be pardoned. But if you are to say that it is your weekly day off when you spend time alone with nature, you are quite likely to attract scornful censure.

There is a third way – a spiritual process where we pray, chant or listen to scriptures. We shall explore this at the end of this section. But, for now, we need to accept and resolve to press the 'pause' button in our lives.

We have to remember, though, that when we suspend our actions for some time to improve our awareness, the mind will habitually threaten us with boredom. The next chapter offers a way to handle what we perceive as boredom in our lives.

SUMMARY

- In the rush of daily chores, we neglect the heart and live in the 'hands' and the 'head' – by performing mere physical actions or by worrying and planning. But real fulfilment comes when we enter the heart, and that begins by first pressing the 'pause' button on our frenzied lives.
- Two ways to improve self-awareness are:
  - A five-minute break amidst our daily chores for conscious breathing (by the four–eight–eight method), which helps us relax and rejuvenate.
  - Spending time with nature, which is healing and can help us to become centred.

CHAPTER SEVEN

Dealing with Boredom

'Give up such petty weakness of the heart and arise, O Arjuna, chastiser of the enemy.'

– Bhagavad Gita (2.3)

I HAVE LEARNT AN effective method of handling boredom while doing my daily duties.

Instead of grabbing my smartphone and watching meaningless videos to entertain myself, I have come up with two action plans. First, I pause and just breathe, and tell myself that it is okay to be bored. Then I ask myself this question: What do I really want in life?

Although I do have a clear sense of purpose for my life, I tend to forget it at times, especially when intense administrative issues plague my mind and I get lost in the myriad details of various projects I am involved in. However, as soon as I remember the intent I have for living, I come back to life; I am excited.

If an activity that I know is aligned to my purpose appears dull on a certain day, I ask myself again what my purpose is: Why am I doing what I am doing? How will this specific activity help me?

I have composed a two-line rhyme that best describes my intention. As soon as I hum it in my mind or even aloud, my life in general and the moment in particular are invigorated, and I find myself raring to go. This is a simple way to improve awareness and help reconnect with my intention for doing that task. As a result, I return to my work with a sense of resolve.

Let's say you go to work daily and have set a goal of earning a million dollars. It's entirely possible that on some days you might forget your goal, or find your job unattractive. Or you might find yourself agreeing with a colleague who is moaning about how life sucks. At that time, your mind could regret your decision to earn all that money; you might even feel despair. It could happen that one morning you wake up and find yourself wondering what the hell you're doing with your life. The last thing you want is to go back to a soulless job. But your mind tells you there is no choice because you need to earn money or get that promotion.

Thus, your day has begun with you feeling helpless, and you are now ready to avoid taking responsibility for your situation. Irritability sets in, your relationship with your family or spouse is under strain, and you feel sick going into work. To mitigate the pain, you may then drown yourself in social media, movies, liquor or drugs. The cyclones in our inner world are persistent; you could be thrown off course from happy and productive living because of a little thought that slithers into your mind and then turns into a blitzkrieg.

To break this disconnect, you need to become aware of your purpose or remind yourself of it. But it's best to do this exercise twice.

The first time you ask yourself what your objective is, your mind could go blank or even protest against such prodding. But if you pause and reflect in a relaxed state, your answer could be, for example, that you need the money so that you can buy a bigger house.

Come back to the question a second time after you have answered it the first time, and ask yourself this: What is the need/value/principle that I seek to serve by having a bigger house?

In response, you might tell yourself that you seek to make

your family happy. So what you realize now is that making your family happy is important to you.

This little question–answer session will help you in two ways.

Firstly, on the days you are not motivated, connecting to your vision will make you more resolute and thus help you take charge of your situation. The difference is between feeling empowered and feeling disempowered. Earlier, it was a pain to go to work, but now it's to please your family.

Secondly, remembering the value of why you're doing what you're doing will help you see that there may be other options available to achieve a certain goal, or there may be smaller goals you can achieve while you are on the way to achieving the big one. It is reassuring to know that one has choices available and one's back isn't pressed to the wall. Isn't it that feeling of despair and helplessness that gets us down so often? When we feel like giving up, if we have something smaller or more achievable to encourage us to go on, then we're more likely to continue our mission.

Working with the example I used above, there are other smaller ways to make your family happy. For instance, you could take them out for a meal or on an excursion to the park nearby. While you give them joy in these smaller ways, you can continue to work on the bigger goal of getting that house you want.

It's our conscious connection to a purpose that helps us move forward during the dull, pointless moments of life. In fact, it is this that gives meaning and purpose to our lives. After the Indian cricket team's 2007 World Cup debacle, the media severely criticized the players. Sachin Tendulkar was distraught and planned to retire from cricket. His brother, however, encouraged him to keep playing. His approach was simple. He asked Sachin what he valued most. Sachin said that he wanted to contribute to the game of cricket and win the World Cup for his country. As he reconnected with his purpose merely by voicing it again, he rediscovered his motivation to play. Eventually, four years later, he helped the team lift the World Cup.

COPING WITH DIFFERENT EMOTIONS

Often, setbacks throw us off course, and if we're not anchored to a goal, we may even slip into a depression. Without an aim, we focus only on pleasure, which is a fleeting experience. One moment we are happy, and the next moment a different emotion consumes us, soon to be replaced by yet another one.

I find emotional fluctuations among humans best exemplified by the weather conditions in England. During my regular visits to that country, I'd often go on long walks in the countryside and would experience heat, cold, rain and dark clouds, all during a 90-minute walk. Similarly, the mind can experience different yet equally strong emotions one after the other.

Although happy feelings are most welcome, they don't always enter the mind. Sometimes we are anxious; at other times, we are happy or worried or angry or fearful. What's more important at such times is to connect to a purpose and rise beyond the passing feelings that come and go. And if we connect to a mission higher than ourselves, we'll easily navigate the phases of boredom in our lives. Ralph Waldo Emerson's inspiring quote says it best: 'The purpose of life is not to be happy. It is to be useful, to be honourable, to be compassionate and to make some difference.'

Thus, in order to counter the boredom that can affect us, it is important to have a purpose in life to keep us focused and interested. Cultivating certain healthy habits helps us achieve this. The next two chapters offer a variety of good habits that can be easily cultivated.

SUMMARY

- To organize your mental space when you are bored or confused, ask yourself this question twice: What is the value/principle/need that I seek to serve with this activity?

- A conscious connection to your values not only helps you to transcend boredom but also keeps you motivated to pursue your goals, and offers alternatives to the 'boring' activity.
- Just as different weather conditions exist, various feelings come and go. But you can stay focused on your values despite the fluctuating weather 'within'.

CHAPTER EIGHT

Three Keys for Self-mastery

'In this endeavour there is no loss or diminution, and a little advancement on this path can protect one from the most dangerous type of fear.'

— Bhagavad Gita (2.40)

ON 23 JUNE 1757, Robert Clive confidently marched to war with his small army in Palashi, a village in Bengal. His army of 3,500 men was about to face Nawab Siraj-ud-Daulah's imposing army of 60,000 men.

As expected, the conflict ended in a few hours. But the historic Battle of Plassey threw up a surprising result: Robert Clive took over Bengal with little resistance. For a single man in Clive's army, there were 17 soldiers in the opposing camp. Besides, the Nawab had better cannons. Yet he lost the battle. Shocked and bewildered, he escaped with his life but was soon arrested and killed by Clive's men.

What went wrong?

The Nawab's commander-in-chief, Mir Jafar, had been bribed by Robert Clive; he was the enemy in disguise. Mir Jafar, along with the Nawab's infantry, had betrayed their master. The British East India Company took over Bengal and soon all of India would be under its subjugation.

A good army has to be equipped with the latest weapons, and ample arms and ammunition. But it also needs to work with intelligence. One tactic used in war is to employ spies to weaken the enemy. A known enemy is relatively easy to confront, but the attack is more lethal when it comes from *within*. When the enemy is undetected, he can wreak greater havoc.

INNER TRUTH VS. ILLUSION (MAYA)

As we attempt to scale the ladder of success, we could declare a war against our own lower nature. This 'lower nature' is understood by various traditions. For example, it is known as maya, illusion, in India, and as 'mito' in the Mexican Toltec belief.

Maya is the energy that pulls you away from the 'true north' principles. Your internal compass directs you to your own unique set of values; these beliefs represent who you are at the deepest level. Yet, you stray from them because of maya.

Maya is the power that gives strength to the mind and the intelligence to rebel against our own deeper interests. We seek happiness and success, and yet many of us fail and remain ever dissatisfied. Why? Because maya, like Clive, is confident and usually has the last laugh. She has our key men – the mind and the intelligence, or our internal Mir Jafars, on her side. She is determined to keep us entangled in material pursuits while our souls hanker to live by virtue and principle. The war is real as daily temptations and distractions threaten to pull us away from our goals.

Maya's agents often go unnoticed. They usually appear as friends, but diligently plant bombs of doubt and dissension *within* us. If we are unable to see the evil ploy of the enemy, we'll be thrown off our path. If caught and exposed, the spies become ineffective; that is, if we are mindful in our daily activities, we'll catch the enemies within. If we are not attentive, we'll imagine the Mir Jafar-like mind to be our friend. And, soon, we'll be vanquished.

Therefore, if we truly want to release ourselves from the clutches of the mind, it is critical that we spend time with ourselves and improve our self-awareness by asking probing questions about the self. The first-century Roman philosopher Seneca had appealed to human kind, 'We should every night call ourselves to account. What infirmity have I mastered today? What passions opposed? What temptation resisted? What virtue acquired? Our vices will abort of themselves if they be brought every day to the shrift.'

A good way to apprehend the 'enemy' is by cultivating the three keys enumerated below.

KEY 1: ATTENTION – RECOGNIZE WHAT MATTERS TO YOU

Attention improves your awareness, and helps you examine your mind. It enables you to see how the mind works in all kinds of complex ways, often unknown to you. The first task in becoming aware is to connect with yourself, to find out more about yourself and who you really are within. So start by asking yourself these questions:

- What do I really want in life?
- Who am I?

Write down what really matters to you, and here I am speaking in terms of values or principles. Is it the principle of sacrifice or humility or gratitude – or maybe integrity or truthfulness – that represents you? Surely your inner voice – the conscience – speaks to you, at least sometimes, about your role in this world. Your contributions are not only unique but precious. You are indeed special, and you can leave behind a legacy. Ask yourself what *you'd* love to do and what you really want to offer to the world. When you become aware of who you really are and what really matters to you, you've taken the first big leap towards connecting with yourself.

Don't worry if no one around you is asking these questions. It doesn't matter; this is about you, and you are allowed to connect with yourself. This is your life, and only you can take responsibility for it. These are questions that will actually change *your* life as you start working with them. Even if you have small, ordinary dreams like spending more time with your family or learning a new skill, and don't really worry about the big picture, you must still practise focusing your attention on yourself. Ask if the work you are doing right now feels right to you or not. Do you really want to do this? And is it worth it? That's awareness in practice, at your own unique level.

If you are someone who has a bigger vision for the world beyond yourself, then list the various things that you could do to help you connect with your life's aspiration. At this stage, don't worry if your present schedule makes it impossible for you to do these things. Just imagine if you had no constraints of time, relationships or resources, and you could do what you wanted. Assume for the time being that all your other needs are met. You are now independent. If you could do what really matters to you, what would that be? As I suggested earlier, write down your answers to these questions.

Self-awareness is the first big step in developing self-mastery. To know who you are is the best discovery you can make about yourself.

Mankind may praise Columbus for discovering America, but your self-discovery is no mean achievement either. Begin the voyage now and spend time with yourself. You could go to the mountains for contemplation, but even if you live in a city teeming with millions of people, where vehicles emit fumes, cars honk all the time, trains bustle with huge crowds, and there are no mountains, forests or rivers for you to relax around, you could still discover yourself. All you need to do is to pause! Stare at the vast sky or simply close your eyes and listen to your breathing.

I live in a monastery that is densely crowded. It's in the heart of Mumbai – a city buzzing with over 20 million people and 28,000 humans occupying every kilometre of space. But we find tranquillity in our daily chants. Chanting is just an example – you could sing and dance alone, write, laugh – just break the drudgery of your life and connect with yourself.

Once you know what you want, you will also become aware of the activities that will help you to achieve your dream. If you have listed even a few activities that align with your vision, you are ready for the second step.

KEY 2: IMPROVING YOUR SELF-WORTH AND SELF-CONFIDENCE

Keep the list of the activities you want to focus on in front of you for daily reference. You can pick at least one activity each day to work on. Let's say exercise or yoga is a part of the list. When you do yoga, you can feel blessed in the knowledge that it's in accordance with your innermost purpose. That very moment, you'll begin to feel worthy. Perhaps appreciating friends and expressing gratitude is another thing on your to-do list. In that case, call a friend and thank her right this instant! Doing the things that align you with your life's purpose will help enrich you, slowly but surely as you keep adding to the emotional balance in your personal internal bank account.

I can almost hear you say 'I am so busy, I don't think I can do all of this.'

I understand, but all it takes is five minutes to align to your purpose. Tomorrow, you can add another five minutes to your schedule. Start each day by looking at your list, and do what you can to get closer to practising it. It's the little things that you want to do that are your true wealth. These things alone will make you peaceful. The more we live in a state where we are at peace with ourselves, connected with the quiet inside us, the more effective we'll be on the outside.

Let your life be determined by *your* vision and values. Don't let the opinions and judgements of others manipulate you. When you do more of the things that help you define who you are as a person, you will find that it will begin to matter less and less whether the world recognizes you or not.

It is not sustainable to depend exclusively on the glories you find in this world because the same human beings who put you on a pedestal can also pull you down. They may deposit 'money' into your emotional account, but their capacity to overdraw is also a reality. And, if that happens, it could affect you in very many adverse ways. So it is always better to earn your own 'money' instead of living on borrowed funds, for the interest you pay will be abnormally high!

If others appreciate you, it would be like a few thousand rupees have been added to your emotional account and you can gratefully accept the honours. But as you work towards transcending the endorsements of this world, you are energized by a deeper, larger purpose, not the temporary pleasures of worldly tributes.

So ask yourself what will truly nourish you and then do that daily, even if it means doing only a little of it. This daily practice to keep *moving forward* is the critical factor. The next key will help you solidify this habit. This third vital step will ensure you sustain your newly cultivated good habits and remain cheerful.

KEY 3: A MINUTE OF GRATITUDE

If you have done something today that truly resonated with who you are, then before you retire at night, just spare a minute to thank *yourself* for being able to do what you really wanted to do.

How will it help?

You will soon understand that the Universe arranges more time and resources for you to pursue the things you gave thanks for today. Tomorrow, the day after, the next week, month and year, you'll see things fall into place; your life will gravitate towards your larger mission.

Gratitude is the greatest wonder of the world; it not only helps us access more of what we are thankful for, but also plants seeds of positivity in our consciousness. Gratitude feeds on itself; the more we thank someone or something for what we have been given, the more we attract that abundance again and again.

Far from being discouraged looking at the vision of your life, genuine appreciation or thanks for being able to do even a little bit of it unleashes tremendous spiritual energy. You will feel happy, and excited to do more.

Still sceptical? Try this experiment: For the next 15 minutes, write a heartfelt thank you note to whoever you feel has contributed to your well-being over the last one year. If it is not a person, it could be a certain factor or event in your life. Write at least two sentences to thank each person or thing.

THE SELF-OBSESSION TRAP

Recently, I tried this experiment with a group of young couples. I told them to write a 10-minute thank you essay during the middle of my class. They could thank anyone they wished – God, their parents, friends or even themselves. As the participants wrote, one student casually looked out of the window. When I urged him to write, he replied matter-of-factly that such activities didn't work for him. I tried to reason with him for a few minutes, but then left him alone and focused on the others in the room.

A few months later, I received a call from the student in question. He thanked me profusely and said joyfully 'It works!' He explained how it had felt like a drag writing down the good things others had done for him, but he had tried nonetheless. Initially, his mind protested because he felt he had done so much for others and they hadn't reciprocated. It took him a great deal of courage to break the self-obsession trap and really think about the niceness of others.

Slowly, he recalled one person's benevolence and wrote a few sentences thanking him. Then he wrote about another person and, soon, found he was hooked to the exercise. He wrote for nearly an hour and ended up thanking even the sun, rain and trees for what they give with such generosity. He said he had never realized that one could be grateful to nature!

I was very glad to know how this gratitude exercise had transformed him. He continued to do it daily, he said, and even began to view those who had wronged him as his benefactors. It was overwhelming, he confessed, to be able to feel gratitude for those who had harmed him. But in the last few months he was able to see that he belonged to a larger creation and that, in the bigger scheme of things, we are all connected.

Are you, on the other hand, still feeling uninspired or sceptical?

Maybe you are carrying a lot of hurt within and are unable to appreciate anything in your life. If that's the case, you could do with a little self-love. Those starved of love struggle to break the cycle of negative self-talk. Try this exercise: For 10 minutes, write down something wonderful about yourself. Appreciate yourself. See the difference it makes in you. And, if you are still lost, you should approach some close friends to help you.

GOOD ASSOCIATION OR MAKING IT HAPPEN

We need good friends. The association of sincere people helps us examine our intentions. When we reveal our struggles to another friend or confess our shortcomings, we stay humble and the sinister plot of the enemy – the mind – is busted. Let me explain how this happens.

When you have people around who care or show interest in you, you need to practise attention. Giving another person attention means gently being present, with all your senses, to the acts, thoughts and sounds you are interacting with. For example, if a friend talks to you excitedly about his new job and if you calmly allow your senses to receive his joy, concerns or fears, he'll feel connected to you. If, however, you're drafting an answer in your head while he's talking to you instead of simply listening to him, or worse, wondering when he'll shut up, he'll soon feel disconnected from you.

With the right kind of people around you, life can become beautiful. The mind and intelligence will be compelled to toe your line and not the other way round. With the inner world in control, the enemy without as well as within will be quelled with ease.

So, find a good time to sit down and write, to express your gratitude for all that you have. In case you're wondering if you can actually sit down and write again, so many years after leaving school, the next chapter will share a simple method of 'free writing', which will help you address this goal.

SUMMARY

- While marching down the path to success, you will face temptations and distractions that are collectively referred to in various traditions as illusions.
- Maya, illusion, pulls you away from your 'true north' by corrupting the mind and intelligence.
- Three simple methods that can help you arrest maya's downward drag are:
    - Pay attention to yourself and recognize what matters to you. Answer two questions: What is your purpose in life? And what activities will help you live according to your vision?
    - Do little things daily: Make a to-do list of activities that will lead you to your eventual goal in life. Do at least one activity daily. Your self-worth will soar each time you do something that defines your purpose.
    - A minute of gratitude: Be grateful for what you have been given. The more we are able to feel and express gratitude, the more positive energy we attract.

CHAPTER 9

The Magical Therapy of Free Writing

'The beauty of a person lies in simplicity and confidence; so live life for yourself and not for others.'
— Sudha Murty

WHAT ARE THE FEES for the world's best emotional healer? Well, you don't have to pay anything; this healing is free. But what you do have to give in return is your time and honesty.

The unchecked mind can throw us into turmoil in an instant. In fact, such a mind is like quicksand: You get sucked in before you know what's happening to you, and it is extremely hard to save yourself. A negative thought is no different. Each thought triggers a certain emotion within. Worse, the emotional roller coaster that follows negative self-talk is like a landmine — it can explode and destroy your sanity.

This is where something as simple as keeping a journal comes in handy. Writing does help in ending the mind's tyranny. Just pick up a piece of paper and a pen, and write.

It doesn't matter what you write. Write anything that comes to mind, but don't stop for half an hour. As you write, move your awareness from your head to your heart and let your emotions flow through your pen. Don't hold back. Don't worry about grammar and punctuation marks; no one is going to give you grades for your journal entry. This is an outpouring of your emotions on the pages; it's your time with your heart – your true companion in life. Free writing essentially means just writing freely whatever is flowing through your heart. Don't put down the pen even if you go blank. For instance, if you are feeling blank, you can simply write something like this: 'I am unexcited; I don't know what to write. I don't feel like writing, but I have promised to write for the next half hour…'

Keep going and let the muddle clear. Writing helps access a field above the mind – and once you begin to do it you can actually experience magic at three levels.

LEVEL ONE MAGIC

For those confused about how it works, here is a case study that explains the therapeutic benefits of free writing.

Preeti was born and raised in a traditional Gujarati family from Rajkot. She studied law and worked for a small firm in Virpur. When she was 25, her dutiful parents got her married her to a pious businessman settled in Canada. The sudden change in her life – both her marriage and a new place of residence – unsettled Preeti. Although her husband was supportive and sensitive to her needs, she often remembered and missed her parents, friends and the city she grew up in. Slowly, loneliness crept into her heart and threatened to suck the joy out of her life.

That's when she discovered a friend called free writing.

She woke up half an hour earlier than her normal time each morning and grabbed her journal. To set the momentum, she spent her first three minutes writing a thank you note to God for all the experiences she had gone through the previous day. She also thanked the people or events that had been a part of that day. Unknowingly, she entered a space of spiritual gratitude – a perfect antidote for the insidious isolation that threatened her existence. Slowly, 'thank you' became addictive – she couldn't begin her day without thanking five events or people. If, on certain occasions, she woke up late or had urgent household chores to attend to, she'd grow restless. Only when she offered sincere gratitude for the preceding day was she ready to face the challenges of the approaching one.

When a railway engine pulls up, the other coaches of the train follow. In the same way, Preeti realized that if she allowed gratitude to direct her mind early in the morning, then the other activities for the day followed with grace and blessing, just like the coaches.

LEVEL TWO MAGIC

Once she was done with her thank yous, Preeti would write whatever she wanted to – no rules or obligations came with this part of her exercise. On one occasion, she wrote how her life had changed dramatically after marriage. Since she had already entered a zone of appreciation, her mind instantly asked her what *good* her move to Canada had brought her.

Did you notice that the first piece of magic led her to see the positive even in a painful situation? That is the second level of magic.

Preeti wrote: 'There is less noise here in Canada, hardly any pollution, and I have learned to cook so many new dishes, thanks to my guinea pig of a hubby. Poor fellow, he humbly allows me to try all my crazy cooking ideas on him. I miss my mom and have now realized the value of family and the love of my parents...'

She cried as she wrote these lines, but they weren't unhappy tears. Preeti understood that the writing exercise that day had filled her heart with appreciation for the bountiful gifts life had offered to her at every stage.

On some occasions, she wrote with feeling; on other days, it was mechanical. But she kept it going like a tonic you take daily for good health.

Then, one day, Preeti discovered the third level of magic.

LEVEL THREE MAGIC

One morning, while writing, a sudden flood of emotions entered her heart for her husband, who lay next to her, snoring. Soon after she was done writing, she reread what she had written and felt strongly that there was something in her thoughts that begged for further attention. She decided to revisit the pages later during the day.

In the afternoon, she revisited the morning's writing. Suddenly, she found herself pouring all her emotions for her husband into a poem, which she later presented to him. He was deeply moved by her act of sincere affection, and their relationship began to blossom into something deeper.

On another day, it rained the whole afternoon and she saw a Canadian blue jay perched on a sugar maple tree across her window. Inspiration gushed through her, and she wrote another poem. Then, a few weeks later, while she and her husband holidayed in the forests, she was inspired to write a poem on the wilds – she contrasted the natural forests with the concrete jungle she had grown up in Gujarat. She compared the birds' hoots with the honks of the rickshaws on the streets, the fresh air of the woods with the pollution in Indian cities. This poem surprised her the most – she could scarcely believe she had so much talent in her. Her husband encouraged her to publish her poems. Soon, she started blogging and became active on Quora and Medium. com. Three years later, she was counselling hundreds of young men and women in creative writing.

She looked back and wondered about the magic that had permeated her life. She confessed she never knew she had a poet in her, and was truly amazed at her discovery.

This is the most exciting magic of free writing. It reveals to you things you don't know about yourself.

FROM THE HEAD TO THE HEART

American novelist Flannery O'Connor said, 'I write to discover what I know.' Writing answers the questions that you are afraid to ask, and also the ones you've asked all your life. You know the answers, and writing helps you know that you know the answers!

A critical factor in this discovery is your authenticity – it's the heart that counts, not the head. Unfortunately, we live in a world that eulogizes perfection, praises external beauty, and sets external barometers for our internal journey. But there is more to our lives than what the world outside acknowledges. We are first accountable to ourselves. Therefore, don't think of others at all while writing about your feelings. Don't let the approval of others motivate you to write; it should be your own need to connect to your deeper self. Don't let the world's judgements of what is right and wrong stifle your growth. You need to trust yourself and write with abandon.

'Let go, live free' is the mantra for journal writing. The freedom and connection you experience are real, the joy spiritual, and the growth constant.

Although we can call such transformations magical, they are real. And, as Preeti discovered, there is more to our lives than our minds. Meeting aspects of your real self over something as simple as a journal entry is an experience worth having!

You may ask, 'Why does this magic appear elusive in *my* life? Why do I find it so challenging to do the right things?' The answer could lie in your pocket!

SUMMARY

- 'Free writing' means to just write – let everything from the head and the heart pour onto the pages.
- As the muddle inside the mind clears, three benefits emerge from free writing:
  - Loneliness makes way for a life of gratitude and blessing.
  - You gain the ability to see positivity even in painful situations.
  - You discovering your talents and abilities.
- The key factor in free writing is the heart, not the head. Authenticity matters more than anything else.

CHAPTER TEN

Smartphones and Foolish Humans

'The characteristic traits of pure consciousness are: Complete serenity, clarity and freedom from distraction.'
— Srimad Bhagavatam (3.26.22)

SINCE WORLD WAR II, we've heard about Weapons of Mass Destruction (WMD). This term had quite an impact across the world: While it made some uneasy, it made others feel secure and many were proud that their country was in possession of these weapons.

Since the early twenty-first century, the acronym WMD has come to mean Wireless Mobile Devices; and thanks to Apple, Samsung, Sony, HTC and a dozen other world players equipped with high-speed 4G mobile broadband, we now have 2.6 billion people on this planet using smartphones. And what do we do on these gadgets? Check messages and emails, browse the Internet, attend to calls and so on. Over 40 per cent of smartphone users suffer from nomophobia, as in no-mobile phobia – the anxiety of being disconnected from friends and family. People now need their mobiles near them even when they're in the shower or having sex!

Perhaps a better meaning of WMD now is Weapons of Mass Distraction. We now have all the right technology available, but it probably exists for all the wrong reasons.

THE COST OF TECHNOLOGY

Loneliness is the cost of this technology, and it has now become an epidemic. There is an expanding body of work that suggests a direct link between the increased use of smartphones and the growing percentage of loneliness. A study quoted by John Cacioppo, the director of the University of Chicago's Centre for Cognitive and Social Neuroscience – who has been studying loneliness for over 20 years – states that nearly 20 per cent of Americans felt lonely in the 1980s, but in 2010 the figure was closer to 45 per cent.

An experiment will reveal to you the mind–mobile phone nexus in your own life.

WEEKLY FASTING DAY

In traditional monasteries, monks fast once a week; on the designated day they don't eat cooked food and grains. They do this to spend more time in prayerful introspection. The modern variant of this culture could be fasting from our mobile phones.

Fasting gives rest to your digestive system; the body releases toxins, and you feel an overall sense of wellness. Interestingly, when animals are sick, they refrain from eating.

Just as these tips improve your external well-being, the occasional fasting from smartphones will bring immense benefits to your internal health. And, just like animals, if you feel 'sick', then get smart quickly and keep your smartphone aside. A lot of mental jumble will get flushed out of your system, and you'll feel an overall sense of peace. If 24 hours of fasting from your mobile feels impossible, try a six-hour fast and see the difference for yourself.

WHAT'S WRONG WITH THE 'SMART' PHONE?

Actually, there's nothing wrong with the phone itself, but there's something seriously wrong with our addiction to it.

There are at least two reasons why a smartphone can be so addictive.

If you reach for your phone because you're lonely, this gadget – with all the content that is instantly available to you – is *not* the answer. You need to connect with the real world, with people, with life. The electronic world is merely a virtual world.

Secondly, a kind of urgency grips one who is in possession of a gadget, because you know that you can access information from anywhere in the world with just a few clicks. A single tap of the screen could connect you to someone in Alaska! It's easy to see why this gadget in your hand is so attractive.

But look at the flip side too: Since you have a smartphone and can access just about anyone, and any information whenever you choose, you tend to think that this makes you efficient and the phone can solve all your problems, including personal ones, for there are websites and blogs that talk about everything, from relationships to sexuality to medical problems.

But life's complex issues – despite all the material available online – aren't going to be solved through your phone. Addressing the real and deep issues in life requires time, human involvement and effort; after all, quick fixes don't work in interpersonal conflicts or in complex communication problems. Since the phone gives you an illusion of control or access, you may wonder why you are unable to quickly sort out nagging personal issues with family or friends. These problems need patience, forgiveness, reflection, prayer and grace – the more subtle aspects of life are in play here. But if you are used to making hurried attempts to address all problems you could drift further away from what you seek.

Keep your phone away and spend quality time with your loved ones. Yes, I know it seems hard to put away something that provides you with a virtual reality, a high-speed life where emoticons, messages and instant responses suck out of you your ability to pause, introspect and connect. But the truth is that it's not efficiency – doing things right – but rather effectiveness –

doing the right things – that will enable you to experience deep, fulfilling relationships.

British comedian David Mitchell aptly explained our plight when he said, 'When the phones first appeared they were so cool. Only when it was too late did people realize they are as cool as the electronic tags on remand prisoners.'

I live in a monastery in Mumbai with over a hundred monks and we serve a community of over 5,000 members. Twenty-nine-year-old Rajeev is an active member of our congregation and he has a candid story to share.

'I wondered why I was generally restless and agitated. My life was like that of any other man my age. Besides, I was financially stable and my domestic life was not that bad. Then why, I wondered, was I irritable all the time. My wife would complain that I wasn't like that when I married her. She accused me of changing a lot in the last few years.

'I got my answer one evening when we drove to a programme in the western suburbs of Mumbai.

'We were travelling in a tempo with 20 monks from our monastery and I was coordinating the drive, a class at the venue, dinner and the drive back to the ashram. As the monks silently chanted, their thumbs flicking their beads or spoke softly among themselves on the way there, I felt a sense of peace wash over me. I couldn't help contrast this with the terrible traffic on the streets where drivers honked, swore and cut lanes dangerously to get to their destination.

'I knew I had to ensure our host and a team of other organizers were ready with the necessary planning for the event. I repeatedly called a friend from my mobile phone, only to explain that we'd take another 45 minutes to get there. Then, I called another friend, and asked him if the flowers and gifts were packed. Then, another call, and finally we reached our destination.

'There was more action and running around at the programme. We left late at night. On our drive back, once again, I was on my gadget – calling or texting someone, watching videos and listening to music. In the midst of this, I caught the eye of one of the monks, who seemed to be enjoying himself at my expense. He smiled at me, sitting

relaxed in his seat, I smiled back at him and he just said one word that blew me away: "RELAX."

'At that very moment, I felt as if a lightning bolt had struck me.

'The monk came over to me and said, "I've been observing you through the evening. I know you had to get many things done, but, honestly, what's troubling you now? Why don't you relax? The programme is over and we are going back to the ashram."

'I sat frozen, my mind blank. I knew he had hit the bull's eye. In just five seconds, I discovered the answer to a problem that had been plaguing me for years.

'I had never relaxed all those years. I thought being busy was not only a sign of my sincerity but was also cool. Through the rest of the journey I chanted with the monks and did a few simple breathing exercises.

'The following day, I reflected on what had transpired and realized that all the frantic phone calls for the programme were absolutely unnecessary. If I had planned in advance and learned to delegate, I could have been peaceful on the day of the event. Moreover, I realized that till a few years ago we never had mobile phones, and I remembered organizing college festivals and holiday tours with my friends without all the frantic phone calls and messaging.

'It's just the culture; everybody is doing it; so I too felt I needed a phone. I also needed to make desperate phone calls and check on everything. But that evening was an eye-opener.

'I now check my phone only three times a day, and I am more productive than ever before. This may not be practical for everyone; my wife has a job where she always needs her phone. But even she has decided to keep away her phone once a week. And our lives are peaceful. We now have more time for ourselves and our kids. My wife recently joked that she is happy I have divorced my former wife – the mobile phone.'

THE ENCHANTING CAPTOR

The electronic screen is captivating. Often, at airports, the news screens invite waiting passengers to see the 'breaking news' and even if you don't want to your head instinctively turns towards the screen. There's nothing wrong with that, except that it's just another distraction in your outside world that serves to take you away from yourself. And if you are someone who is already disconnected from himself, or dealing with painful mental health issues or other stresses, you urgently need to connect with your inner world. Fancy electronic or digital gadgets have a grip on people to the point that they can't think for themselves anymore.

We pride ourselves on creating machines, computers and phones that can now think like humans, but it's a matter of shame if humans begin to think and live like machines.

Smartphones are deceptive; we don't even realize we are their victims. No one imagines that a gadget can be a cause of anxiety. That's because we assume we are smart and *we* are in control of the phone. Little do we know that it's the phone that has trapped us. I guess that's why it's called the smartphone!

Like Rajeev, I've met hundreds of men and women who are able to celebrate life more simply because they have said no to Facebook and other social networking sites at least once a week. Your mind could protest and tell you that these apps are 'free' and you should make the most of that. But are they really free? Read the next chapter to find out about the heavy price you pay for spending excessive time on your gadgets and online.

SUMMARY

- Humanity has moved from weapons of mass destruction to wireless mobile devices to weapons of mass distraction!
- While smartphone sales have swelled in the last decade, loneliness has also increased.
- A weekly fast improves our bodily health. Likewise, fasting once a week from mobile phones improves our mental well-being.

CHAPTER ELEVEN

The Myth of Free Wi-Fi and Social Networking Apps

'An intelligent person does not take part in the sources of misery, which are due to contact with the material senses. O, son of Kunti, such pleasures have a beginning and an end, and so the wise man does not delight in them.'

— Bhagavad Gita (5.22)

A BOARD OUTSIDE A restaurant announced: 'Eat as much as you want – we'll make your grandson pay for it.'

Popatlal thought he was an intelligent man and since he wasn't even a father, this was his chance to lap up the offer. After he'd devoured three pizzas and five bowls of ice cream, he wished he had a spare tummy. His tongue craved for more, but his stomach protested. He resigned to his fate and reluctantly rose to leave.

Just then, the waiter presented him with a bill for Rs 1500.

'I thought you said it's free? I mean my grandson will pay for it, right?' asked Popatlal, surprised.

'Yes, sir, sure,' said the beaming waiter. 'This one though is your grandfather's bill.'

THE COST OF FREEBIES

We often hear the phrase: 'There are no free lunches.' The expression originated after American bar owners in the mid-nineteenth century advertised a free lunch to those who purchased liquor. It was an attractive offer – you could eat as much as you wanted if you brought one drink first. But the unwitting customers didn't realize that most of the food was heavily salted, and they spontaneously craved more liquor to neutralize the salt's effect.

Everything comes with a price – even what you think is free has an invisible price tag attached to it. The only way you can enjoy a free lunch is if you *control* your appetite! For those who can't regulate their senses, if you're excited by a 'free' offer, it means you just can't see the invisible price. And you may end up having to pay with what is most precious to you: your freedom.

I once watched a cartoon that showed a man take a jibe at his Wi-Fi: 'I am using you because you are free' to which Mr Wi-Fi mischievously says, 'And I use you, sir, because *you* are free.'

WhatsApp, Twitter and Facebook are free, and we shell out hours of our precious time in exchange for their services.

So, are these social networking apps really free?

No, they're not. This so-called freedom makes the mind a prisoner and we don't even know it. We can't think beyond gadgets – most people's eyes are riveted to their devices the entire day, failing to appreciate the beautiful, expansive sky above their heads. From self-realization, we've moved to selfie obsession.

A drug pedlar first gives a free sample to an unsuspecting teenager. Soon, the lad gets hooked to it. We've heard of young boys rob and murder to get enough money to buy drugs. The 'free' offer eventually proves very costly. Many teenage delinquents are victims of this freebie propaganda. Often, what comes as free, targets your choice and freedom. The aim is not to get your money, but *you*!

VALUE YOUR CHOICE

You are a consequence of all the choices you make. Every single action you take or decision you make, no matter how tiny, determines your character and personality. We need a sense of self-worth to say 'no' to things that deceive us, and 'yes' to actions that nourish us. How can we allow someone to rob us of our freedom to make choices?

'Time is money' is a well-known maxim, and to have more of it, one needs to be diligent and careful. If we spend precious hours updating statuses and uploading selfies, how will we ever upgrade our consciousness? Good things in life don't just happen automatically. One needs to invest time consciously on activities that add value and meaning to our lives. And then, slowly, we blossom to a fruit- and flower-yielding tree; we add meaning and value to others' lives as well.

WHY WE WASTE TIME

Lokesh was a highly talented man, addicted to smoking and drinking. He chose to work as an office boy in a small government office. Although no job is menial and we should respect dignity of labour, Lokesh was a misfit there. While in college, I had seen his leadership and business talents in full display during fairs and college festivals. I knew he had a bright future ahead of him. After college, we parted ways and years later, when we met again, I was disappointed to discover he hadn't tapped into his talents. His leadership talent seemed to belong to a past, alien life.

Later, I learned he was an incorrigible gambler as well. His friends had tried their best to reason with him, but he was unwilling to change and declared that he was helpless. He resigned himself to his fate as his bad habits dragged him further and further down. Eventually, liver cirrhosis took his life when he was just forty years old.

Martin Luther King Jr. once said that if we have nothing to die for, then we have nothing worth living for. Lokesh had chosen a job where he failed to see a vision more substantial than the mere trifles of his life. That made it easier for addictions to get him. If we don't have a worthy ambition or goal to focus on, and by that I mean something that helps us connect to our true selves, it's easier to get hooked (and stay hooked) to temptations.

If Lokesh had a passion for living or if some values had helped him define himself, then bad habits wouldn't have held sway over him. Even if they did get him he would have within him the desire to resist and change, at some point. But here was a man who had lost the will to live and share his gifts with the world. His mind became his worst enemy and it devoured him like the Unforgivable Curses employed by Lord Voldemort.

Compare Lokesh with your archetypical neighbour, the 17-year-old Chunky, who is fascinated by and hooked to Facebook and WhatsApp. How is he any different from Lokesh? If the teenager discovered his talent in music, dance, writing, tennis or the crafts and, under the loving guidance of his elders, had a passion to pursue, do you think he would have found time to spend hours messaging his friends about what he ate for lunch, who he met the previous or what cologne he was using at the time?

Also think about what would help Chunky find fulfilment and contribute better to society – pursuing his abilities or forever comparing himself to others and, as a result, feeling miserable? Not everyone loses themselves, thankfully, but the threat posed by the digital world is very real. As an adult, if you find it hard to put your phone away and focus on work, for example, you can imagine how vulnerable a teenager with a phone in his hand is.

Any time that you spend on absolutely anything means you are giving away a part of your life that you'll never get back. An hour spent on the Internet is your best gift to it. Therefore, it's time we ask ourselves: What am I getting in return for giving Facebook or WhatsApp the best gift I have, which is my time, a part of my life?

WHATSAPP: HANDLE WITH CARE!

'A man who dares to waste one hour of time has not discovered the value of life.'

– Charles Darwin

Two different incidents that happened over a period of six months taught me the need to practice caution on social media groups.

In an ordinary housing society in a crowded suburb of central Mumbai, there were children playing outdoors all day as their summer vacations were on. One morning, Kripa, a 13-year-old girl, accidentally fell from the terrace of the six-storeyed building she lived in. Although in a coma for almost a week, she miraculously survived with multiple fractures and, in fact, recovered fully within eight months. The family members were naturally deeply anxious during this period.

Since the girl's mother was not aware of social media or even WhatsApp, she was spared more agony that would have come her way otherwise. During the accident, while the neighbours rushed the girl to the hospital, a group of well-wishers – not yet baptized by the selfie and smartphone culture – gathered around to protect the mother.

They initially told her that Kripa fell while playing and had to be rushed to the hospital. While driving the panicked mother to the hospital, two women who were fully aware of the seriousness of the matter, consciously downplayed the situation. They cushioned the grave news as the mother repeatedly wondered aloud about what exactly had happened to her daughter.

As the day passed in the hospital, the ladies gradually revealed that Kripa had fallen from the first-floor balcony. Later they told her it was probably a fall from the second floor balcony. Other women from the housing society came to spend time with the mother through that day and the next, assuring her that everything would be fine. Slowly, the mother figured out that things were probably worse than had been let on and, over time, her cognitive system braced itself to bear the news.

Slowly, each day they came closer to the truth and, by the time her daughter regained consciousness, the mother had learned about the eighty-foot fall. While the doctors worked tirelessly, and relatives and friends prayed fervently, the mother survived what could have been an incredibly traumatic time thanks to the way the community rallied around her.

But imagine if she were active on WhatsApp? She would have probably had to face the shock much earlier. Different groups on WhatsApp would have posted the news and photographs of the accident, and given her all the details of the tragedy right away.

The next story I want to share with you is about a 35-year-old lady from Mumbai, Sheila, a baptized veteran of the social media culture, who was rudely awakened to its dangers one day. By her own admission, she was addicted to WhatsApp, and she would take selfies or update her Facebook status every half hour.

Pritam, her husband, worked 2,000 kilometres away in Kolkata and flew back home to his family every alternate weekend. One morning in Kolkata, while he was out for his morning walk, a speeding car hit him and he passed away instantly. Even as his colleagues and friends wondered how to break the news to his wife, when Sheila woke up that morning, she got the news in an extremely insensitive manner.

Sheila's daily ritual was to check Facebook and WhatsApp first thing in the morning to read funny jokes and enjoy videos. She believed the best way to begin a day was to laugh every morning and what better way to do that than to check out the jokes her friends shared freely on WhatsApp. This morning, though, she ended up reading about her husband's death on various WhatsApp groups and saw messages that said things like 'Let's pray for the departed soul.' She became hysterical with shock and horror.

It's been a year since the tragedy as I write this. Sheila is recovering slowly from the deep depression she had slipped into. The incident not only revealed to her that she had more virtual friends than real ones, but also showed her that the phone isn't quite the blessing that people think it is.

YOUR ACHILLES' HEEL

A big reason people reach for the 'comfort' of their phones is to avoid loneliness. But we don't seem to understand that this is a vicious cycle, and a superficial Band-Aid can't heal our deep insecurities and fears. What consumes the mind is what controls one's life. We need to choose active, real and meaningful conversations to connect with others; we need to honestly contemplate what is important to us.

We can't discount the importance of social media, but to give it top priority in our daily lives means us that we are handing over the reins of our lives to an unknown power. Greek mythology tells the story of Achilles, who was invincible in battle. Well that was until the day a small arrow hit him on his heel and killed him. At his birth, his mother had dipped him in the Styx, a river that granted immortality to his body. However, the heel with which she had held Achilles as she immersed him in the water remained untouched.

Achilles grew up to be a mighty warrior, dodging weapons hurled by enemies with ease, and winning many battles. In fact, he was declared invincible. But when he was shot on his heel, the only part of his body that was vulnerable, he did not survive. I talk about Achilles so we can look at our own weak spots. Human society has made incredible strides in science and technology, yet this small, poisonous arrow of a time-wasting obsession could be our fatal weakness, the reason for our downfall.

However talented or smart you think you are, you'll have some weaknesses, for we all do. The negative forces inside your mind are as aware of your frailties as they are of your strengths. So when you are inattentive to these distractions, you give power to the forces that work against your welfare. It does not help that one is dismissive of ancient wisdom and the wise sayings of masters; nor does it help when one refuses to tap into the gifts one has.

Often, if you are busy with activities that are incongruent with your talent, you will likely get frustrated deep within, though in all likelihood you will be unaware of this. Since there is no proper engagement for your mind, the Internet – like drugs or liquor – will quickly drag you down.

HEALTHY HABITS

Today, since most of us need these gadgets and applications because of our work or because our communication systems depend on them, we can't avoid them entirely. Still, it's possible to protect ourselves from their adverse effects through some healthy practices.

One practice I have now adopted is to ensure that I don't pick up the phone when I wake up. Most of us reach for the phone as soon as we wake up. The most important activities on rising from bed are prayer, meditation, going for a walk or writing in your journal. These activities are 'mindful'; they help you connect with your inner self and centre you.

There's an ocean of adventure that exists beyond our mobiles. Let's seek these rich treasures by making our lives better without the phone telling us what to. After a life-enhancing experience like exercise or journaling, when I check my WhatsApp, I tend to skim through the messages and only seek out the important ones. Since I spend adequate time in the mornings on activities that nurture me, I have little time left to squander on my phone, or online.

Let's spread goodness around. It's our collective responsibility to educate ourselves and our youngsters to stay away from these gadgets. You are not 'free'; you have many important things to do, and if you flick through the host of messages on your phone quickly and then put it away, it helps you retain control of your life. If your mind cheats you by saying there's a lot of inspiration and wisdom out there on the Internet, let me remind you what Paramahansa Yogananda, India's legendary guru and yogi, said, 'It is not your passing inspirations or brilliant ideas so much as your everyday mental habits that control your life. And your success is hastened or delayed by these habits.'

If the electronic world offers a 'virtual' reality, or a mirage, what is real in this world? If this is a question that comes to your mind, the answer to this lies within you, and spirituality could trigger that discovery. The next two chapters will take you on an inner journey beyond the mind.

SUMMARY

- If you spend hours and hours on Facebook and WhatsApp, it means the social media apps aren't really free because they're using *you*!
- When you pursue your talent and passion, you'll have less time to waste on addictions in general and social media apps in particular.
- Picking up the phone the second thing in the morning is the best practise you could adopt. The first thing could be an activity that centres you, for example, exercise, a nature walk or meditation.

CHAPTER TWELVE

Three Levels of Practical Spirituality

'May noble thoughts come to us from all sides.'
— Rig Veda

Some people imagine spiritual life to be abstract or impractical. Therefore, in order to explore spirituality, it will help to first understand the difference between the material and the spiritual realms.

By 'material', I am referring to the physical life, which includes our lives, the daily routines we live out, and even the highs and lows that keep us so busy! Our interactions with 'matter' produce experiences that touch us at the level of the senses and the mind. However, when we enter the space of deeper principles, our experiences are more long-lasting than our sensory perceptions, which are temporary, for example, the short-lived pleasure of eating a pizza.

Spirituality is something that goes beyond matter; something that invigorates and energizes us in a deeper way. When we connect to an undying or unchanging phenomenon within us, we begin our spiritual journey. For example, you may watch a video on your laptop, but the images that flash on the screen are 'unreal' in that they have no veritable existence. A slightly 'higher' level of reality would be a live song and dance that you see on a stage, or your interactions with people and situations. But, on closer examination, you will realize that although these exchanges are real, they are a temporary situation.

Beyond all of these ephemeral states, there is a reality that doesn't change. The experiences you have in nature, for instance, say on a mountain or by the sea, inhabits a space of timelessness in relation to your few years of existence in this body. The peace you experience in nature or during meditation is a higher reality, for you are connecting to an undying self in these deeper states, and this is the real you.

Thus when you rise beyond your bodily or material circumstances, you are seeking something that survives the fluctuations of this world. That search and discovery is 'spiritual'. Let's discover this deeper experience by expanding on one such principle in this chapter -- that of gratitude. The way we practise a simple 'thank you' can give us a spiritual experience, especially if we raise the level of gratitude from our temporary lives to a reality beyond 'I'.

Below, we will explore the three levels at which we can practise gratitude, and thereby take our experiences from the material to the spiritual level.

LEVEL 1: AN EXPERIENCE OF GRATITUDE

Write down five things that you are deeply thankful for. The experience of happiness induced by the practice of gratitude is obvious. Most people remain disconnected and find spiritual joy inaccessible because they only see the negative aspects of their lives. But this first step of thanking our good fortune is a liberating experience; from despair we slowly enter the space of celebration.

This celebration is real, unlike the enjoyment of temporary pleasures. A positive celebration of life is more fulfilling than a denial of suffering through sensual experiences. Although the focus here is still the self, it's healthier because we aren't running away from our inner discomfort but focussing on our blessings.

There are people, however, who tap into a richer source of contentment by taking their spiritual experience to the second level.

LEVEL 2: MOVING FROM 'I' TO THE OTHER

After expressing gratitude for what you have in life, you could try thanking people not for what they have done for you but for who they are, and for what they do, independent of you. Here, the focus is on the wonderful qualities of the other person; his or her *being* is a cause for celebration. It's a person-centric approach that is an effective way to tap into divine happiness.

Focusing on the self is important; in fact, it is essential. But we are still at the level of 'I'. Now, if we appreciate others for their existence and their activities in general, we begin to touch a higher dimension of happiness. 'There's more to life than me and my worries' is the message we send the Universe. That's when we also learn to see that our existence and miseries are tiny compared to the vast amount of goodness in this Universe. It's a paradox: We are aware of our insignificance, yet we feel deeply satisfied.

Once you have developed a healthy habit of thanking others – friends, strangers, things, experiences or events – you are ready to enter the third level of spiritual experience.

LEVEL 3: MOVING FROM THE SPECIFIC
TO THE ABSTRACT

The third level is when we move from thoughts of the self and others to the force that governs us all. We have learnt to appreciate ourselves and others but now we will reflect on what actually moves us all to act or be who we are.

I once thanked a friend in our monastery for his consistent cooking services. I was one of the hundred-plus fortunate monks who were the daily recipients of his benevolence. As he heard me out patiently, I realized my appreciation was about how his cooking had given *me* satisfaction and nourishment. I was not focusing on him but on myself.

I decided to take my appreciation to the next level: rather than looking at how my needs had been satisfied I turned my attention to him. I wondered aloud how he managed to balance his tight schedule and the special skills that he had developed over time. His humility and willingness to learn was a great inspiration. As I openly praised him, I could sense that he felt happy and encouraged and that I had entered a spiritual space. My worries and anxieties seemed insignificant in comparison to the joy this other person was now experiencing.

I then decided to take my appreciation to the third level. I asked myself these questions: Who is responsible for him being so wonderful? What is the energy that is common among the many good men and women of this world? What is this force that inspires people over millennia to contribute, love and sacrifice for the welfare of others? How does goodness spread in a world even as hate and anger threatens to destroy it?

Slowly, as I focused on these questions, I could see my consciousness enter a larger world – from I, to him, and then to It or the real Him. This force is known in our as Krishna or God. I was now connecting to God, or the spiritual being, who inspires goodness in me and others in this cosmos.

I, HE AND GOD: A DAILY APPLICATION

Practically speaking, this is what I did: At the first level, I thanked my friend for what *I* had received from him; then, I expressed gratitude for the person that *he* was; finally, I thanked *God* for providing food for countless living entities daily. From the tiny ant in my room to the huge elephants in Africa, some force is providing nourishment for all. I thank that Force, and I enter a spiritual space almost instantly.

This experience of the heart is real. 'In giving, we receive' is an old maxim and we discover its truth when we raise the bar of our living at the second level.

It's time we realize we are all connected in one way or an other. As the astrophysicist Neil deGrasse Tyson once said, 'We are connected to each other biologically, to the earth chemically, and to the rest of the Universe atomically.' Let's recognize this connection and celebrate it – this is what spirituality is!

If I indeed belong to this Universe, and there's a force beyond what my mind can comprehend, how do I access it? As Chapter 13 will reveal, the wisdom of the past can solidify our relationship with God and the Universe.

SUMMARY

- Material life refers to daily living with its share of worries and pleasures. Spiritual life refers to a deeper level of existence – a space of introspection, connection and gratitude to the Divne.
- There are three levels at which one can practise a spiritual life:
  - Level 1: Thankfulness and gratitude helps us move from despair to a zone of celebration.
  - Level 2: Appreciating others for who they are, independent of what they do for us, allows us to connect with the larger humanity.
  - Level 3: Connecting to the energy that infuses everyhting around us with goodness – 'it' or 'God' or 'Him' – the divine consciousness takes us to a higher level of spiritual awareness.

CHAPTER THIRTEEN

The Echoes of Books of Wisdom

'The Bhagavad Gita is a living creation, rather than a book, with a new message for every age and a new meaning for every civilization.'

– Sri Aurobindo

'THE ENEMIES ARE ONLY 50 yards from us. We are heavily outnumbered. We are under devastating fire. I shall not withdraw an inch, but will fight to our last man and our last round.'

These immortal words of Captain Somnath Sharma resound in the heart of every Indian. Captain Sharma was the first recipient of the Param Vir Chakra, India's highest military recognition, which is awarded for exemplary acts of valour during wartime.

On 3 November 1947, Sharma's troops were surrounded on three sides by 700 Pakistani infiltrators. Realizing the city of Srinagar and the airport were vulnerable if they didn't check the advances of the enemy, Sharma bravely rallied his troop of merely 20 men, even though he was injured, with one arm in a plaster.

Disregarding the fact that they were outnumbered, Sharma's men managed to hold back the enemy for six long hours until reinforcements arrived. In the end, the captain and his gallant men lost their lives, but not before they eliminated over 200 enemy soldiers. The enemy lost their impetus – Captain Sharma's extraordinary bravery had saved the day and the city.

No one could recognize Captain Sharma's badly mutilated body. They eventually identified him because his pocket contained a copy of the Bhagavad Gita – he had carried the Gita in his pocket since he was a teenager. Lord Krishna's teachings to Arjuna had inspired this young 24-year-old to live and die for a cause beyond his own – the service of his country.

Our ancestors carried a silent wisdom gathered from their own experiences, coupled with the teachings of their forefathers, who lived closer to nature. When we listen to the timeless wisdom of these sages and practise them in our own way, we make an amazing discovery. These principles hold true even today. After all, these principles, sanatana dharma, are regarded as the eternal wisdom of Hinduism, transcending time and space.

When we read from these books with an open mind, we enter a deeper space within the self. Things fall into place in our beings; we develop clarity, and also discover our 'aha' moment. Poet and Pulitzer Prize winner Amy Lowell said, 'Books are more than books. They are life, the very heart and core of ages past, the reason why men lived and worked and died, the essence and quintessence of their lives.'

Henry David Thoreau was an unabashed admirer of the Bhagavad Gita, which he claimed shaped his consciousness. Thoreau found similarities between Walden Pond, a lake in Concord, Massachusetts, and the Ganga, which flows in India. He appreciated yoga and the Indian diet of rice. So absorbed was he in his spiritual pursuits that, minutes before his death, he found a deep union with the Divine as he declared, 'Now is the time for good sailings.' He meant that he was now embarking on a happy afterlife journey to the realm of eternity. He lived for just 44 years; yet, his works shaped the destinies of the nineteenth and twentieth centuries. Leo Tolstoy, Mahatma Gandhi and Martin Luther King Jr, among many others, confessed that they were deeply influenced by Thoreau's writings.

MODERN 'GURUS' AND ANCIENT WISDOM

One of the most influential self-help gurus of the twentieth century was Wayne Dyer. I was impressed by his writings. He said he was a self-made man and confessed he sought spiritual wisdom from many sources, acknowledging them in his later works. Nisargadatta Maharaj, the Indian guru of non-dualism, was his teacher. Dyer was also influenced by the Shiva Advaita doctrine and the teachings of Swami Muktananda. Further, he was enriched by the Chinese philosopher Lao Tzu and his book *Tao Te Ching*. What is important to note is that Lao Tzu appeared 500 years before Christ, and the Advaita doctrine was given by Shankaracharya in the sixth century. Rather than dismiss the theories of the past as irrelevant dogmas, Dyer sought the essence of these teachings.

Don Miguel Ruiz is another excellent example of how ancient teachings can profoundly influence us to attain spiritual enlightenment. Born in Mexico, he became a neurosurgeon and practised medicine for several years. One day, he met with a near-fatal car accident and, stunned by the close shave, sought answers to the mysteries of life. He returned to his rural Mexican setting and learnt humbly from his mother and other teachers the wisdom they had gathered for generations.

Eventually, he left the field of medicine and discovered his own path to awareness. He studied the ancient Mexican Toltec wisdom, which had originated in 2000 BC, and developed a deeper understanding of the Universe, life and the human mind. He then penned his realizations in the form of a book, *The Four Agreements*, which sold over 7 million copies, and remained on the *New York Times* bestseller list for over seven years.

THE THREE Rs: HOW TO APPROACH
THE WISDOM OF THE PAST

It is said that if a man is potent and the woman fertile, their union will give birth to a child. Similarly, when the wisdom of the past meets a sincere student who is ready and receiving, the combination will create a volcanic explosion of wisdom and ecstasy.

The key here is openness – the willingness to be influenced. If you are ready to learn, the timeless principles in these teachings will echo with your own inner wisdom.

Once, I was travelling with two friends to a holy place of pilgrimage. It rained very heavily that evening and we were stranded in our hotel rooms. Unable to go out, we decided we would connect with the ancient wisdom available to us. One of us played on a small speaker a 1966 lecture by Srila Prabhupada, the foremost proponent of Bhakti yoga during the counter-culture movement of the 1960–70s. The class lasted for over an hour, and the three of us listened silently without judgement and bias.

Later, as the rains continued unabated, I asked my two friends if we could recall what we had heard in the lecture. Instinctively, my friends dismissed my idea; they said that they may not remember anything at all. I insisted we try and, over the next hour, whenever one of us recalled a point, the other's memory was jogged. Like this, much to our own surprise, we recalled the entire class. Then, one of us suggested we share what we relished about the class. Once again, we discussed the entire lecture for an hour, each of us adding some other thought that we had heard or read elsewhere that resonated with the point we had heard that day.

Outside the window, the rain showed no sign of letting up. I suggested we discuss what we could do differently in our lives based on what we had learnt together that day.

Thus were born the three tools of connecting with the ancient scriptures: Recall, Relish and Resolve.

Now, we spend some time after our stipulated reading or listening to just recall what we have studied. Then, we write down or share what we have enjoyed about that day's lesson. And finally, we reflect on what we can add or change in our lives for the better, based on the wisdom we have received.

So, if you're looking for ways to change yourself, here is

something you can start today. Your opportunity for 'spiritual' or inner growth is always within your reach; it is not something remote or inaccessible to you.

Earlier, as an apprentice in the ashram, I was keen to read and gather more information as quickly as possible; I wanted to maximize the results with minimum effort. Later, I realized the virtue of chewing and digesting spiritual food, rather than simply swallowing loads of information that don't actually bring about any transformation in my consciousness. My mentor in the ashram often says, 'Any fool can know. The point is to understand.'

Now, whenever we read or hear sacred teachings, we pause to reflect; we share what we have learnt, what we liked and what we propose to live by based on our study and learning from the pages of these revered books.

That evening in the hotel room, we unanimously felt that the mundane gossip and political news of this world paled in comparison; we were relishing the taste of a higher plane. The joy of our inner journey is substantial and the news of this world can't give us the same experience. Rumi aptly put it when he said, 'Yesterday, I was clever, so I wanted to change the world. Today, I am wise, so I am changing myself.'

SAM'S TRANSFORMATION THROUGH SOUND

There is serenity and timelessness in spiritual subject matters and this true story explains the principle better.

January 1985:

Sam thought it was a queer sight. He felt a strange sensation running down his spine. Drawn like a piece of iron towards a magnet, he approached the elderly gentleman in the remote village of Manikpur in Uttar Pradesh, reading an ancient-looking book while standing at the entrance to a grocery store. The man uttered exotic chants in a rhythmic metre. It was pleasing to the ears. Meanwhile, a middle-aged man sat at the counter, waiting for customers and a young boy of four played in the courtyard.

'Excuse me, sir, what are you doing?' asked Sam.

The old man's reflexes were slow. He looked at Sam, lowered his chin and adjusted his glasses. The harsh north Indian winter seemed to make no difference to him. 'I am reading the Ramayana,' said the man, his toothless smile enchanting Sam.

'And who is this man at the counter?' Sam said.

'That's my son. He now manages the shop while I chant the whole day. You see, I am retired,' the man explained.

'And that child?'

'Oh, he's my grandson.'

Sam asked the old man what the Ramayana was and he answered in broken English. He chanted a few verses in a melody and metre that Sam found beautiful.

Sam basked in the presence of these mysterious chants, as the rustic setting soothed his heart. 'This was far out,' he thought. 'Nothing like what I have ever felt in Manhattan, the most densely populated borough of New York City.' His trip to India had borne fruit that day. He had long desired to find out what went on in Indian villages, and what cultures and traditions kept families bound together. And here, in Manikpur, he had experienced it first-hand.

Decades passed…Sam grew older. He desired to visit India once again.

January 2015:

Sam was in India again. He recalled his memorable experience from 30 years ago and decided to visit Manikpur once more. Sam was now 55 years old.

In the village, he rubbed his eyes in disbelief. 'Have I travelled back in time?' Sam panicked for a moment. He saw an old man reading from the Ramayana, while a middle-aged man sat at the shop, and a small child played on the porch. 'What year is it anyway? No, it can't be,' he thought as his heart swelled with emotion. He felt nostalgic, but how could it be the same scene again?

He went near the man. 'Excuse me, sir, what are you reading?' Sam felt he was replaying the same conversation.

The old man – who didn't seem to have aged at all in these 30 years – lowered his glasses, smiled at Sam, and replied in broken English. 'I am reading the Ramayana. You see, I am retired, and my son now manages the shop. And that's my grandson playing. He is lovely, isn't he?'

Sam felt a sudden chill.

'Er…but how old are you anyway? I mean, who are you?' he asked.

The man spoke slowly. The old man Sam had met 30 years ago was dead and gone. He learnt that the elderly man reading the Ramayana now was the son who had once taken care of the shop. The man at the counter now was none other than the child who had been playing freely on the veranda back then. Now, he was a man, handling the shop's customers.

Sam understood that even though a lot had changed, on a deeper level, everything was the same. Nothing had really changed.

Sam saw an eternal continuation of a spiritual culture, something that he had missed during his earlier visit. He could now see the scary contrast between this way of life, and the frantic pace of the modern life he lived.

The steady culture of listening and absorbing the scriptures has remained in some of these Indian villages. On the surface, reading the same scriptures and chanting the same holy names may seem boring, but now Sam could see that peace and stability comes only from consistently performing the same spiritual practices, day in and day out.

A sudden realization dawned on Sam: There is so much clarity when we are connected to an eternal space of transcendence – a place where nothing changes. The more the world outside of us changes, the more we need to embrace that which doesn't.

Sam went back to the US and made a daily habit of reading the scriptures. He learnt to 'listen' and receive wisdom; his prayers were now more meaningful, and he could experience divine guidance in his life.

DISCOVERING THE SOLUTIONS TO PROBLEMS

As each year brings with it ever new challenges for humanity – tumultuous relationships, mental health issues and stress, climate change, pollution and terrorism – we rack our brains for lasting solutions. Interestingly, the answers are already there. There is nothing new for us to discover that the Universe hasn't already arranged in its eternal time cycle. We simply need to access those answers.

Many of my friends in the spiritual tradition I come from have been serving for over five decades now, and, for inner nourishment, they chant mantras and attend regular classes. Yet, they are ever relishing new sweetness in their busy and eventful lives. Life in the monastery will appear dull if we simply live by the external activities we do. But, for a discerning observer, absorption in Srimad Bhagavatam, the Ramayana and other sacred books, and holy chants helps one enter the spiritual space.

Yes, our problems and practical issues remain for now, but by connecting with the spiritual energy, we enter a zone beyond the world of the mind. That solves a bigger problem and helps us transcend the heavy block of our worries.

From that vantage point, you can see your problems for what they are and also understand how you can face them.

According to me, the most important gift that the wisdom of the past gives mankind is the serenity to accept the vicissitudes of life. This composure amid the chaos in our lives, and in the world beyond, is called Acceptance, which I shall be talking about in the next section of this book.

Starting from the next chapter, we shall explore the power of humble self-acceptance and the tools to develop it.

SUMMARY

- Over millennia, the principles of wisdom have remained the same. True wisdom endures.
- The method to approach eternal wisdom is:
  - Principle: If we have openness to receive the knowledge, we will discover these teachings echo our own intuitive understanding.
  - Tools: Learn, like and live by the following:
    - » Recall (Learn) – remember what you read, and reflect on the subject.
    - » Relish (Like) – connect to a phrase, example or teaching that resonates with you; spend some moments with it.
    - » Resolve (Live by) – ask what you can implement today and right now, something that will enhance the quality of your life.

SECTION 2

Acceptance

'These people are not the cause of my happiness and distress. Neither are the demigods, my own body, the planets, my past work, or time. Rather, it is the mind alone that causes happiness and distress and perpetuates the rotation of material life.'

— Srimad Bhagavatam (11.23.42)

CHAPTER ONE

From Denial to Acceptance

'It's better to do your job imperfectly than another's perfectly.'
— Bhagavad Gita (18.47)

A THIEF ONCE DECIDED to steal a temple's golden bell. But there was one problem. The moment he lightly touched the enormous gong, it made a loud sound. Removing it would mean the bell would clang a great deal, and the villagers would certainly discover him. What was the way out then? He decided to put cotton in his own ears. He reasoned that if he couldn't hear the sound, neither would the villagers.

Many live in this sort of denial. A friend, who is a chain-smoker, told me that giving up cigarettes wasn't a big deal for him. He could quit any time he wanted; he claimed that he didn't because he didn't feel like it. He is a classic victim of denial. To be in denial is to refuse to recognize the truth, although it's evident to everyone else. And the worst part is that it doesn't feel like denial when you are the one doing it.

As long as we refuse to accept the reality, we remain slaves to the mind. The solution is simple: Acceptance.

WHAT IS ACCEPTANCE?

Acceptance is the act of consenting to receive the present moment; and it is therefore the most effective way to arrest the mind's rant.

When you accept that you are addicted, you stand a chance of getting cured, but when you deny your weakness for something, for example, cigarettes, the mind takes you deeper and deeper into that illusion. If you cannot accept something, you are actually granting the mind the permission to continue that activity. It is simple really: 'If you will not acknowledge that something exists, how can you seek to change it?

On the other hand, you might worry that in accepting what you are doing, you may actually be giving yourself the licence to continue. Let me assure you that that is not what I mean. Accepting something – for example, unhealthy behaviour like an addiction – doesn't mean that you are meant to be happy about it or are seeking to justify it. It means that you have accepted your vulnerability and can now seek help for that problem.

When self-talk is unhealthy or painful, just stop and accept that you are in pain. When you are anxious about your strained relationship, just admit that you are in fear: 'I accept I feel insecure and fearful.' The moment we accept our situation, we save ourselves the misery of denial, anger and bargaining.

We seek happiness in a world that guarantees us misery. If we accept the reality that this world is a place of suffering, then our expectations will be more realistic. It's only then that we can seek alternatives. Otherwise, we keep doing the same things over and over again and just get frustrated. Our predicament is best echoed by Albert Einstein, when he said, 'Insanity is doing the same thing over and over again and expecting different results.'

THE PARADOX OF ACCEPTANCE

The Buddha was once approached by a bereaved woman who had lost her only child. She was desperate for him to bring her child back to life. He heard her out patiently and then deferred the miracle by assuring her that he could revive her son, but she would first have to get some rice from a house that had not seen death.

She immediately rushed to a nearby house. While the hosts gladly parted with some rice, they also confessed that about two years earlier they had lost their parents to old age. Then the lady hurried to another house, where the man had lost his wife the previous year in an accident. Soon she discovered that someone had died in each of the houses she visited. Slowly, the reality dawned upon her, and she was able to come to terms with the inevitability of death. The Buddha had taught her the lesson of acceptance with compassion.

It's a strange paradox that while enlightened beings declare this world to be an abode of endless misery, they are blissful. On the other hand, despite all the 'new age' resources available to us for inner peace and healing, be they books, workshops, retreats or classes, and all the 'positive thinking' we are told to practise, many people are still drowning in alcohol or drugs to forget their unhappiness and stresses.

Facing your misery and accepting it helps you transcend the situation. Imagine that after performing various medical tests, a doctor reveals the many complications a patient has with his kidney, liver and heart. How will the patient react? If he gets upset with the doctor for giving him 'bad' news and seeks another doctor's advice, will that really help him? Whereas, if he accepts the reports and prepares for the battle ahead, he will be more peaceful. Once we accept our limits, there is a good chance we might go beyond them.

WHEN ACCEPTANCE IS NOT ACCEPTABLE

When we talk about acceptance, I would like to make it clear to you that this cannot be an absolute principle. There are certain situations in life that you should not accept – for example, if you are a victim of abuse and domestic violence. Please do not accept abuse, violence and disrespect; seek help immediately.

Acceptance refers to the principle of not resisting the flow. If you are abused, and you have been timid all your life, you now need to accept that you've got to stand up for yourself and fight it out.

Acceptance does not mean that we resign ourselves to our fate; it is about quietly moving forward in life with grace and dignity. For example, when I am stuck in a traffic jam, I catch myself resisting my situation because it means that my schedule is thrown out of gear. I can react with irritation or anger, refusing to accept the situation I am in. But there's nothing I can actually do to get the traffic moving. I merely need to accept the situation with quiet grace and focus on being present on other things, or on simply being present in the moment. I could listen to lectures, look out of the window or call a friend, but the point here is not to resist what I cannot change at this point. Otherwise, all I will succeed in doing is feeling frustrated and miserable.

I rise early each day and have a list of things to do. Yet, sometimes when I wake up late, I catch myself regretting that I wasted my precious hours sleeping. That's when I make the conscious choice of accepting myself the way I am. It's okay to wake up late today. Let me offer the best I can now, and make do with what I have, I tell myself. As I stay level-headed with acceptance phrases, I get the strength to reorganize myself and carry out my responsibilities for the day to the best of my abilities.

Denial is the way we try and 'control' what we cannot control, and that makes matters worse. It would be so much easier to learn from our mistakes if we were not busy resisting or denying them.

Therefore, let's learn how to practise acceptance in the coming chapters.

You may still be wondering if acceptance is some sort of weakness or indulgence. Maybe your mind is saying to you: But if I accept myself the way I am, I'll get complacent. I won't be determined enough to improve. The next chapter challenges the concept of misdirected determination.

SUMMARY

- Denial means a refusal to accept the truth or reality of a situation.
- Acceptance is agreeing to receive the present moment, just as it is. For example, if you feel fearful and insecure, just accept that you are fearful. You can then deal with your anxiety more easily.
- It's a paradox that enlightened beings know this world to be a place of misery, yet find deep happiness within, whereas many who champion the cause of positive thinking are unable to find happiness.
- If you are a victim of abuse of any kind, then acceptance means to let go of the internal resistance, seek help and justice.

CHAPTER TWO

Human Being or Human Doing?

'Just as God is perfect and complete, all His creation – this phenomenal world and the creations thereof – are perfect, complete whole.'

– Ishopanishad

IN THE MAHABHARATA, THE warrior Salya instructs Karna through the story of the crow and the swan.

The crow ate and ate and grew fat. He was boastful and often teased the swan, saying, 'You are good for nothing, a bland, white-coloured bird.' He was determined to defeat her in a flying contest. He proclaimed, 'I have learnt a hundred unique ways of flying gracefully.' He pushed the swan to race with him, and when the swan accepted the challenge, off they flew together.

The crow demonstrated the upside-down flying technique, and he also twirled and showed off a special triangular pose he had learnt just for this competition. Soon, they were gliding across the ocean. Slowly, the crow began to comprehend that he was no match for the swan. The ocean seemed endless and while the crow felt himself weakening, the swan continued to fly majestically. Finally, the crow slipped and fell into the water. The swan flew close to him and exclaimed, 'Oh, what an amazing pose! You never told me about this. Is this one of your hundred ways of flying?'

THE TRAGEDY OF DETERMINATION

If I am a crow, but desire to fly across the ocean, my determination and self-motivational tools are unlikely to help me. That's because I have the inherent strengths and existential limitations of a crow. However, for a swan, both the vision and determination to fly over the sea seem reasonable. The crow needs the awareness and acceptance of his inherent strengths and limitations before unleashing determination.

If my efforts in life are an offshoot of the awareness and acceptance of being who I am, then my determination is likely to nourish me.

If I am resolute about studying medicine when I love engineering, I will likely get frustrated very quickly. Determination is a limited resource; if I use all of it in doing what is not the real 'me', I invite stress and fatigue. On the other hand, if I situate myself in the 'be', if I know who I am – a poet – then my determination will accordingly nourish me in my romantic pursuits.

Many 'do' things hoping they will 'be' happy by their doing. However, if we are happy in our real state, in the state of 'being' (acceptance), then we'll be directed to 'do' from a more profound state of awareness. Whatever we do then will nourish our very souls.

And there are others who prefer to live in the 'have' mode. 'I don't "have" this, if only I "had" this, I could "do" that and then I would "be" happy…' They are directed by the 'have' syndrome. They lament, hanker after things and live in regret.

BE, DO AND HAVE

The three states of existence are Be, Do and Have.

If we learn to 'be', all other things will blossom from this state.

Generally, determination is a short-term currency; it fizzles out with the power of time. I am determined to run 10 km every day, but my capacity is only 2 km. I may run the first kilometre with great enthusiasm, but soon I'll collapse because time will beat my determination.

The crow needs to first accept that he is a crow. Then his determination will accordingly direct itself to life-enhancing targets. Since he tried to be a swan, all of his conviction was merely a pathetic show of 'doing'. He likely lived a life of regret – a life of 'have'. Instead, if the crow had chosen to 'be' a crow, he'd have been happier and inspired all the other birds to 'be' what they were.

Don't let others cheat you; don't let the propaganda get to you. If you are a crow, be gracious and accept it, and offer the best of you to this world. The world needs beautiful crows as much as it needs swans. 'Be' yourself and accept God's unique gifts to you with gratitude and grace.

You may protest and think that being a crow is so pointless. But the reality is that you can contribute immensely even as an ordinary person – if only you have authenticity. We'll explore this in Chapter 3.

SUMMARY

- 'Be', 'do' and 'have' are the three states of existence.
- If we situate ourselves in our natural state – 'being' (acceptance) – then we can contribute – 'do' – better.
- Many also live in regret because the core of their existence is 'have'.
- When a crow tries to be a swan, all action will eventually lead to frustration. But if he accepts that he is a crow, he'll be happier, be able to do his best and inspire others to 'be' what they are.

CHAPTER THREE

Do You Seek Greatness or Authenticity?

'Stop, where are you running? The real things lie inside. You might miss them if you keep looking outside.'
— His Holiness Sachinandan Swami

IT WAS THE WEIGHTLIFTING event at the London Olympics in 2012. Wu Jingbiao was distraught. On a live television interview immediately after the incident, he cried and was deeply sorry for having shamed his motherland.

Wu had just won a silver medal for China.

Wu is one among 30,000-plus athletes that Beijing trains for winning the gold in the Olympics. From the age of five, boys and girls undergo rigorous training, cut off from their family and any sort of fun, so that, one day, they can prove they are the best. China's desperate attempt to derive soft power through Olympic supremacy has come at a hefty price – inauthentic lives and personalities. China has become a big factory that produces medal-winners and, ironically, this obsession has brought pain to most competing athletes.

Four years later, in the 2016 Rio Games, China won even fewer gold medals: from 48 in 2008 to 38 in 2012, and now just 26! But a 20-year-old called Fu Yuanhui became an online sensation after she won the bronze in swimming. She was thrilled because she had broken her previous record. In a candid interview, she expressed joy at having surpassed herself. She instantly won millions of hearts, and back home in China, her authenticity attracted many admirers.

In life, like in sports, real heroism is to compete with oneself. Pierre de Coubertin gave us the Olympic creed: 'The most important thing in Olympic Games is not to win, but to take part, just as the most important thing in life is not the triumph but the struggle. The essential thing is not to have conquered but to have fought well.'

Fu Yuanhui had lived this principle in her swimming event, and that instantly resonated with Olympic fans worldwide. Her childlike innocence came as a breath of fresh air for Chinese fans – she had redefined the Chinese athlete.

OBSESSION WITH GREATNESS

Our obsession with success and fame blinds us to the simple and ordinary pleasures of life. Our reckless hunger for achievement takes away the simple joy of being.

Take, for instance, the strikingly different examples of Michael Phelps and Ian Millar.

We remember Michael Phelps as the most successful Olympian of all time, with 28 medals, while hardly anyone sings praises of Ian Millar who, at the age of 65, at the 2012 London Olympics, represented Canada in the equestrian event for the tenth time! Yes, you read that right – he has taken part in the Olympics for over four decades, whereas Phelps – often considered the greatest swimmer ever – retired at 29. After the 2012 Olympics, he declared, 'I'm done, I'm finished, I want to be done with swimming, and don't want anything to do with sports any more.'

Phelps was also arrested a few times for driving under the influence of alcohol, and USA Swimming suspended him from all competitions for six months. At 19, he won his first gold medal, and, 10 years later, with over 75 medals in various championships, he was a living legend. Yet, his passion took a toll; he didn't want to be in the sport, he didn't want to be alive. Yes, he contemplated suicide. Today, he has recovered and is helping many others overcome depression. In an interview, he confessed that the feelings of wellness and the healthy emotions he was experiencing were now 'light years better than winning the Olympic gold medal'.

Contrast Phelps' frustrations with Millar's words when, at age 61, he won his first Olympic medal – a silver – in the 2008 Games. When asked how he felt about being a sports icon, Millar dismissively said, 'I don't know what they are talking about. I just do the best I can…I love it all; I love every moment of it. For me, it's all fun.' For most sports fans, Phelps is a hero – and there's nothing wrong with that; he richly deserves to be so – but it's the likes of the silent Millar who fulfil Pierre Coubertin's ideals.

The fact that the world celebrates Olympic champions is essential because it inspires many to struggle and succeed. But if you aren't a champion in the world's eyes, you could still be a hero in your own right. And if the world showers no glories on you, should that be a matter of concern? I believe it is alright to be who you are, without being concerned about the judgements of other people.

BE HONEST – KNOW YOUR CAPACITY

In the Ramayana, the monkey soldiers of Sugriva analysed how they would jump over the ocean to reach Lanka. Their goal was to enter Ravana's kingdom and get news of Sita. However, each one of them was honest about his abilities. One soldier said he could jump only 20 yojanas (the Vedic calculation of sea miles) out of the 100-plus distance. Another monkey claimed he could leap 50 yojanas. Angada said he could cross the whole length, but wasn't sure if he'd have the strength to return. Finally, the veteran Jambavan reminded Hanuman about his Herculean abilities. The giant superhero of the Ramayana then not only jumped across the ocean, but he did it in style.

Often, we are encouraged by self-help gurus to unleash the 'Hanuman' within us. Motivational speakers assure us that we all can, like Hanuman, do what is impossible. Self-belief is the motto. Never shy away from aiming for the sky. You can win; success is your birthright. These are some of the inspirational phrases we hear, pushing us to achieve great heights.

But the uncomfortable question that no one seems to answer is this: What if you are not Hanuman, but an ordinary soldier who can only jump 20 yojanas? What if you are Angada or even the small squirrel that carried pebbles to build the bridge for Lord Rama? There are no temples for squirrels or Angadas, or even Jambavans, who help others discover their potential.

LET'S CELEBRATE OUR ORDINARINESS

Next time someone tells you to unleash the Hanuman within yourself, ask instead if he can reveal to you your own capabilities, your inherent strengths. Those who help us reach our potential are our friends. TV serials and movies portray lifestyles of rich and successful people. The glamour bug strikes a poor man living in a chawl; unconsciously, he may aspire to live like the stars he sees on screen. His aspirations turn unrealistic, and his ambitions take him further away from his core self. Eventually, he either becomes depressed because of his inability to get what he wants or resorts to unethical methods to try and fulfil his desires.

Is there a place for ordinary beings on this planet? Can you be the rank and file in the Lord's army? One cause of depression is when people take up challenges beyond their capacity; inevitably, they falter, within or in their external lives.

I once met a cricket coach who shared his success story of having coached many boys who had got into the Ranji Trophy and the national teams. I pressed further, and he revealed how millions of young boys all across the country aspire to be like M.S.

Dhoni and Virat Kohli. He cited examples of teenagers travelling long distances daily to learn from good coaches. From small towns to the maidans of Mumbai, these boys carry heavy kits on their shoulders; they also have grand dreams. Many of them don't even make it into their state team, leave alone the national team. When these boys fail to get ahead in this highly competitive sport, some eventually pick up vices and harm themselves.

The same principle holds true in other fields. A manager might dream of becoming a CEO or a lawyer might hope to become a judge not because they want to but because they feel the societal pressure to be the best in their fields. However, one can be an average person and still be useful to other people! A schoolteacher can give as much, if not more, than a cricket champion or a famous actor. What matters more than the kind of work we choose to do is the authenticity we imbue it with. If we do what we love, it will be hard to do it badly! In following the truth of the heart, one can find happiness and even success. It's in our authenticity that we discover success and happiness.

LEAVING BEHIND A LEGACY

To leave behind a legacy, you don't need recognition; you only need the desire to contribute. An Indian saying instructs: 'The rivers don't drink their water; the trees don't eat their fruits. The clouds don't eat the crops to which they give water, and the endeavour of good people is only for helping others.'

C. Rajagopalachari – popularly known as Rajaji – had the honour of being India's first and last Indian-born governor general. He was a distinguished lawyer and statesman, an accomplished scholar and writer, and the recipient of India's highest civilian honour, the Bharat Ratna. His contributions to society were dependent neither on the office he held nor on his clout. It was only his service that defined him. In the decade following India's Independence, he made lasting contributions to polity, art, music, literature and social causes.

When Lord Mountbatten had to leave for England to attend a family wedding, Rajaji was appointed as acting governor general. In the few months that he stayed in the royal palace, he lived simply – he washed his own clothes, polished his own shoes and ate quietly. But it was his abilities that attracted the leaders of the nation at that time, and they asked him to take on more responsibilities.

In 1990, Richard Nixon, the former president of the US, released a memoir in which he mentioned that one of the most dramatic influences in his life was Rajaji, who spent a few minutes with him one afternoon, 36 years earlier. During that meeting, the two men discussed, besides other issues, spirituality and reincarnation. The profound effect of these ideas shared in the brief exchange helped Nixon shape his speeches over the next three decades. John F. Kennedy too remarked that Rajaji had the most 'civilizing influence' on him; he declared that Rajaji had precision, clarity of thought and elegance of language.

One can be a simple person in life, but a small contribution of goodness – whether it's from a monkey soldier or a politician or a policeman – has far-reaching effects; it can influence society. Ramakant Achrekar gave the nation Sachin Tendulkar, although he didn't play for India himself. Does that reduce his contribution in any way? When I see a grandmother tell devotional stories to her grandchildren and offer them love, I know she is contributing, in reality, as much as Abdul Kalam and Mukesh Ambani. To leave behind a legacy, what we need is genuine goodness, not greatness or pomp.

You may worry about society's approval. Yes, we do have a social need – we are humans, after all. But a few close friends and relatives will suffice for that. To think you are a success only if you are 'someone' is merely social conditioning; it is an illusion at best and self-deception at worst. You can choose to uphold virtue in the face of temptations and champion the cause of truth. Then, whether the world sings your glory or not, you have contributed to the welfare of humanity.

There are plenty of examples of people who chose to defy the conventional path to fame and fortune and chart their own authentic course of life. Chapter 4 reveals an inspiring example.

SUMMARY

- A desperate pursuit of success can blind you to the simple but powerful joy of being authentic.
- Our authentic self is more fulfilling than artificial goals.
- Celebrate who you are, who your authentic self is. Following a path that is not true to you can result in various problems including depression.
- In a war, along with powerful leaders, we also need capable rank and file. Similarly, in society, 'ordinary' people matter as much as saints and statesmen.

CHAPTER FOUR

Transcending Glamour

'Everyone – even the most learned – follows his own nature.
What can repression accomplish?'

– Bhagavad Gita (3.33)

EDWARD BERNAYS IS REGARDED as the father of public relations and the pioneer of propaganda. In the 1920s, when smoking was taboo for women and the general opinion was that only lower-class women smoked, Bernays changed it all. As part of a campaign for the American Tobacco Company, which sought women as its customers, Bernays branded cigarettes as feminist. He organized the famous 'Torches of Freedom' campaign, where women flaunted cigarettes to display their freedom from the shackles of male chauvinism. When these women were asked how smoking would give them more freedom, they said it didn't matter; it was an expression of freedom! Canadian podcaster and author Stefan Molyneux exposed the problem with this way of thinking: 'If you can convince people that freedom is injustice, they will then believe that slavery is freedom.'

MANIPULATING YOUR MIND

People like Bernays have one agenda: to manipulate the minds of others. The way we think, eat, live and behave is not really ours, for we are being conditioned all the time by social influences.

The way out of this mess is to go within, and connect with the real self. If you are centred, if you are at peace within and have a strong sense of self-esteem, another person's judgement or criticism will not affect you. Now you may want to know how one can develop a sense of self-esteem. This takes time as it needs work with the self, but the way to do it is to form a connection with the self. As I discuss in this book, it starts with simple steps, such as making friends with a very important part of yourself: Your mind.

Unfortunately, the physical world distorts our perception of things. It presents an unreal picture, and if we fall for it, we get disconnected with our inner selves. It requires a rare courage to be honest and reject the external and illusory messages we are constantly being bombarded with, temptations that threaten to take us away from our true selves.

DARING TO BE HONEST AND DIFFERENT

Mansoor Khan is a film director who dared to transcend the razzle-dazzle world of Bollywood, to be his own person. In the mid-1980s, Bollywood's reputation took a serious hit. The movies dished out were substandard, the slicks predictable and boring.

Enter Mansoor Khan with new ideas and a freshness that took the entertainment industry by storm. He had new actors, debutant music directors and singers, and *Qayamat Se Qayamat Tak* was the pleasant and welcome change that Bollywood was looking for. The film won the prestigious National Award for the best movie of the year 1988, and numerous other accolades flowed in. After that came *Jo Jeeta Wohi Sikandar* – another box office winner. Mansoor Khan was here to stay.

But his educational background was exceptional, and you might have thought he would have become a professor in the US instead of coming to Mumbai to make films! He had graduated from the Indian Institute of Technology (IIT), and then from Cornell University and Massachusetts Institute of Technology (MIT).

People compared him with his father, Nasir Hussain, and declared that the son's talents had surpassed his father's directorial skills. Mansoor Khan, however, scripted a different story for his own life. He knew his calling was different. Even when his first film was about to be released, he tried to ensure his name didn't appear in the credits. He didn't want the fame of Bollywood because he had seen the shallowness of it all. His father, an accomplished director, had become a prisoner of success. Mansoor Khan, as a teenager, saw his father's inability to cope with failure when some of his movies bombed at the box office. Although he was famous, Nasir Hussain feared he would lose his reputation. Mansoor Khan saw that his father was desperate to keep up his name. Soon, it dawned on him that this sort of fame compels one to live with a wrong identity; one works hard to maintain one's position while being disconnected from one's real self.

Mansoor Khan launched his cousin, Aamir Khan, in his movies, and Aamir went on to become a superstar. Two movies later, Mansoor was established as one of the biggest film-makers in India; and then, he decided to call it quits.

He began to understand the hardships of farmers; he started working with them, learnt about their struggles and bought a farm in Coonoor in Tamil Nadu. He soon settled there, took care of cows, made his own cheese and today uses cow dung–produced energy for cooking at home.

During his rich education, Mansoor Khan had studied economics and energetics. He now read and researched extensively and realized the dangerous path human civilization was treading in the name of growth. He then researched environmental challenges and shared his ideals in his book, *The Third Curve*. The book was a result of his deep study and meditation, developed by living in congruence with his own self and nature. Since then, he has been invited by leading organizations, including the Indian Institute of Management (IIM) for talks on energy and economics.

Today, at 60, he has no regrets about leaving Bollywood. By choosing to live a life true to himself, he has shown us the path to contentment.

The most influential African–American social reformer of the eighteenth century, Fredrick Douglass, made a beautiful appeal to the human conscience: 'I prefer to be true to myself, even at the hazard of incurring the ridicule of others, rather than to be false, and to incur my own abhorrence.'

We are constantly faced with distractions and temptations, and it's not easy to follow our inner calling. Especially when our soft inner voice implores us to be agents of positivity, but our raging minds and senses, influenced by the overabundance of temptations, directs us away from ourselves. Paradoxical as it may sound, our conscience is that still, small voice that is sometimes too loud for our comfort. Yet, if we show courage and determination to follow the right, although difficult, path, we may be pleasantly surprised to see that we reach a beautiful destination. The correct choices always give the right results.

The truth is that you always know the right thing to do. The hard part is doing it. Mansoor Khan has shown us the way.

Now, you may worry that you won't change your career overnight, and Mansoor Khan's method can't work for your life! Chapter 5 addresses the strategy and skills needed to make changes based on the honest acceptance of the self.

SUMMARY

- Social conditioning impacts how you think, behave and live.
- To repair the 'manipulated' mind that takes you away from your true self, you need courage and honesty.

CHAPTER FIVE

Three Keys to Developing Acceptance

'Rise, prepare and win – they are already defeated; just be an instrument.'

– Bhagavad Gita (11.33)

KAMLESH OZA WAS DESPERATE to become a manager in his company. His promotion was long overdue. Anxious months passed, and he sought solace in an overdose of liquor and cigarettes. At last, three years later, he got the coveted promotion but, after a few months in his new position, he confessed that he still wasn't happy. He concluded that he was just not meant for this kind of job.

A spiritual therapist suggested he spend a few minutes daily in prayer and contemplation. A little breathing exercise, journal writing, prayers and significant association with other spiritualists would help remove the confusion from his mind. Within two months, he discovered the cause of his misery – his inability to accept himself the way he was!

As he contemplated and meditated, he realized that, as a teenager, he had taken up engineering in college because his parents had wanted him to. He had been fascinated by history and psychology, but he had felt an acute need to win the acceptance of his parents. During his two-month inner journey, he journaled daily for 20 minutes, which also helped him discover that his parents' constant fights during his formative years had made him insecure. His sense of worth was negatively affected. He now sought approval from his friends and took up a corporate job, even if it meant he was disconnected from himself.

Contemplative prayers and journaling helped him connect with himself and discover that he was a teacher at heart; he loved spending time with children. Slowly, he realized that he'd be a great schoolteacher. While he rejoiced at the prospect of teaching children, his mind shuddered at the thought of leaving his career. His ambivalence paralysed him internally.

THE NEED FOR ACCEPTANCE

For the Kamlesh Ozas of this world, the Chinese philosopher Lao Tzu advised: 'Life is a series of natural and spontaneous changes. Don't resist them; that only creates sorrow. Let reality be a reality. Let things flow naturally forward in whatever way they like.' Kamlesh knew he had always resisted the natural flow; he had denied the 'reality' of his love for teaching.

Our lives are steeped in artificiality; we hardly connect with our authentic God-gifted talents. Instead, we seek to live according to the terms and conditions laid down by others. Kamlesh's spiritual practices gave him a sudden sense of relief, and he was now happy. Nevertheless, life isn't as easy as we imagine and the mind can be dreadfully nasty. Kamlesh began to feel anxious again. The thought of being a teacher was appalling. How could he become a school teacher when the friends he hung out with regularly were all go-getters, flaunting flashy cars, and were productive and 'successful'?

He had undoubtedly improved his 'awareness' in these three months. He knew who he was and what he wanted to be. But a million-dollar question stared him in the face: *Can I accept myself just the way I am?*

'No way, what would your friends say?' his mind screamed at him.

Again a question begged to be answered: Is it really worth doing what your friends are doing simply because you need their approval? And how do you know they won't love you for making your own choices in life? And if they don't accept you the way you are, are they truly your friends?

The answers were clear to him. He simply needed the courage to accept them. Let's look at three keys or steps that will help you learn acceptance.

STEP 1: AFFIRMATION

Kamlesh finally took the big step: He internally accepted himself as a teacher. Affirmations, or positive statements about the self, made in the present tense, helped him come to terms with his true self. This, coupled with prayers and functional social support, paved the way for a new phase in his life.

Many live their lives according to the dictates of others. By the time they realize they too have an individual sense of identity, they think it's too late. Once they know they have a purpose and a dream, another problem invades their mind – that of fear and guilt. 'How can I change now?' or 'Am I being selfish?' are common self-limiting beliefs that plague many people. They may have won half the battle because they have 'awareness', but they can't muster the courage to 'accept' the self.

Affirmation is therefore a critical first in the three steps to developing acceptance.

Here is an example of an affirmation:

I approve of myself, and I accept myself just the way I am. I love myself and I forgive myself.

Sounds strange?

For those raised in a culture of guilt and fear, this could sound bizarre. But for one who seeks freedom from the vicious clutches of the mind, this is the golden key to happiness.

Read the affirmation stated above again. Can you see how Oza desperately needed this? Instead of seeking encouragement and approval from the world that's busy with its own problems, this man thought of encouraging himself. He reasoned that God helps those who help themselves, and so he began to invest his feelings in these statements.

The energy we unleash into these consciously chosen thoughts creates a new reality for us – a truth that incubates in hope and aspiration. The renowned American philosopher Ralph Waldo Emerson said it best, in his *Essays: First Series* (1841): 'The ancestor of every action is a thought.' He declared that one can be rich in the mind with the right kind of thoughts.

And the right thoughts or affirmations need 'energy' to yield results, just as your body needs 'food' to function. This energy comes from visualization.

STEP 2: VISUALIZATION

Arnold Schwarzenegger was a victim of child abuse. His father would pull his hair, him with belts, refuse to understand him and even accuse him of not being his biological child. So intense was the mistreatment that later, when his father died, this young man refused to attend his funeral. Despite the negativity unleashed on him in his childhood, Schwarzenegger went on to become the biggest icon in the world of bodybuilding, winning the Mr Olympia contest seven times. Considered widely as the greatest bodybuilder of all time, says he refused to be broken; each time he faced failures in life, he vowed to rise and be someone extraordinary.

As you affirm, you could spend some time visualizing the reality you desire. Spend some quiet moments where you visualize your life revolving around your desired goal. Many sports coaches encourage their protégés to visualize the game in their mind. A good tennis player imagines her serves, volleys and smashes to gain an inner sense of control before she starts to play the game.

The first reality is within and that later manifests on the outside, often even without our conscious awareness.

Maxwell Maltz in his bestselling work *Psycho-Cybernetics* narrates the case of a World Chess Championship match finals. José Raúl Capablanca, a prodigy with exceptional skill, was sure to win. The young and inexperienced Russian boy, Alexander Alekhine, stood no chance. In their past encounters, Alekhine had not won even a single game against the Cuban legend. Yet, the entire chess world and Alekhine himself were surprised by his stunning victory in a gruelling final, which lasted two and a half months. It was like an amateur boxer defeating a world heavyweight champion.

A lot of analysis has been done on that match, yet a little-known fact is that Alekhine trained for the game differently. He retired to the countryside, quit smoking and drinking, exercised daily to remain agile, played chess 'in his mind' and visualized his success. By the age of 22, he was already among the most influential chess players in the world. Alekhine remained the world champion for 17 years and is widely considered one of the greatest chess players of all time.

Kamlesh did something similar. He imagined he was teaching kids, laughing and playing with them, and sharing exciting stories from the World War II, which held his students in rapt attention. Even if this seemed a distant and vague reality, he found it helpful because it filled his heart with an innocent kind of happiness, the joy of giving what he had.

Many serve selflessly, but are unhappy because they are disconnected from themselves. This may be because they are trying to give back to the world that which they themselves don't really have! Like Oza, you may claim to serve selflessly, but if you are trying to fix a square peg in a round hole, you'll be miserable. However, when you do things that truly represent your inner self, you'll be ecstatic even when your actions are a mere internal visualization.

The happiness of doing what you really want to do is real; it helps you contribute meaningfully to the well-being of others. As Kamlesh began his visualizations, he added a strong positive energy to his subconscious mind. It was a robust expression of his real inner aspirations.

Kamlesh Oza was positive and hopeful as he also began to supplement affirmations and visualizations with small steps.

STEP 3: THE SMALL STEPS

A local NGO needed help with their school in a slum, and they looked for volunteers to teach the kids. Kamlesh had been practising affirmations for a few weeks when he learnt of this opportunity from a friend.

He later confessed that the Universe does help, and things begin to fall in place for us when we practise positive self-talk and visualize what we really want to do. Since he lived the reality of teaching children in his own inner world, he was now ready to deal with the truth even in the outside world. And the offer just fell into his lap.

Often, opportunities come knocking on our door, but we are deaf to them. Strange as it may sound, the most dangerous obstacle to realizing our dreams is the guilt and fear of success. We may think it's our fear of failure that prevents us from getting what we want. But Paulo Coelho, in the introduction to his bestseller *The Alchemist*, offers an alternative insight: 'People make stupid mistakes just when they are on the verge of getting what they really want, and that's because they believe somewhere deep inside that they don't deserve it.' So you might feel saintly that you gave up something that would make you happy, because people around are suffering and they fail to get what they want. So 'I too deserve to suffer' is the deceptive inner dialogue. Many men and women are almost there, yet they lose, because they secretly believe they can't win or they don't deserve to be happy.

Kamlesh too could have quickly become a victim of this. But he won the big battle inside; he 'accepted' himself as a teacher. His visualizations simply reinforced his belief systems and prepared him to face the inevitable reality. He was ready for the challenge;

when the NGO offered him a chance to teach at their school, he grabbed it. He volunteered to teach these children history and psychology on weekends.

This was the small step he took in his journey towards awakening. Soon, weekends became three days a week. Then four, and finally, one day, he quit his job and became a full-time teacher. The change wasn't sudden or painful. He had seen it coming because he had taken small steps towards his inner goal.

Kamlesh's transformation wasn't as dreadful as he had imagined. He was happy not just with the result he had achieved in the end, but even with the process of affirmations and visualization – the little steps he had taken filled his heart with joy.

Happiness, he realized, was in the journey, not just the destination!

But life's journey is filled with shocks and suffering. How do we face them with quiet fortitude? If this is your concern, the next chapter will help you.

SUMMARY

- With improved awareness about yourself, you can find out what is it that you really want in life.
- Three steps to accept yourself:
  - Affirmation: Make positive statements about yourself in the present tense. When you add emotions to these consciously chosen thoughts, you invest energy in them and move closer towards acceptance.
  - Visualization: Live the reality you desire first in your mind. Arnold Schwarzenegger and Alexander Alekhine proved that by first creating a reality in their inner worlds, they could change their lives.
  - Small steps: Start taking steps now, even if they seem small to you, to create the changes you want in your life.

CHAPTER SIX

Seeing Meaning in Suffering

'If you attain the highest, you won't return to this temporary world full of suffering.'

— Bhagavad Gita (8.15)

ROALD AMUNDSEN HAD ALWAYS been attracted to the wilderness. As a young boy growing up in Norway, he desired to be the first man to reach the North Pole. However, in 1909, when two Americans made it to the North Pole, Amundsen was disappointed. Then, he decided to be the first man to reach the South Pole instead. Meanwhile, British Naval officer Robert Scott cherished the same desire and he was supported by the Admiralty.

Who would get to the Antarctic first? While Scott prepared for over 12 years, Amundsen kept his plans a secret until almost the end. As Robert Scott began his journey, Amundsen telegrammed to say he had already begun. Thus began an intense race to be the first man to reach the South Pole.

Dogs, motor sledges and ponies were used by both parties with meticulous planning to journey the 1,300 km. The -40°C weather was no deterrent to either man. Finally, after three months, Robert Scott and his team arrived at the South Pole only to discover a Norwegian flag fluttering there — Amundsen's team had beaten them by five weeks. Scott was shattered, and he wrote in his diary: 'The worst has happened...all my dreams are crushed.' He suddenly found the place awful. Anguished, he began the return journey where rough weather, scurvy, frostbites and the lack of proper support led to each member of his team meeting a tragic death.

One would imagine that although Scott felt crushed, Amundsen would be happy at his historic achievement. Scott became a martyr, but Roald Amundsen was not happy either. He reflected, 'Never has a man achieved a goal so diametrically opposed to his wishes. The area around the North Pole – devil take it – had fascinated me since childhood, and now, here I was at the South Pole. Could anything be more crazy?'

MISERY DEFINED

Once, an elderly holy man in the village of Vrindavan gave me an interesting definition of misery: Misery is to get what you don't want, and to not get what you want. Both Scott and Amundsen experienced this. Amundsen's sobering words simply confirm how most people are unable to accept these universal laws – many are tragic victims of non-acceptance.

Although we wish to get everything we want and not experience what we don't want, we know that it's not possible. As the Booker Prize winner Chinua Achebe put it graphically: 'When suffering knocks at your door and you say there is no seat for him, he tells you not to worry because he has brought his own stool.'

Therefore, all our endeavours are to maximize what we want and minimize what we don't want. That keeps us busy. To find happiness, which for many is simply an attempt to reduce misery, we use technology, money or individualism; we compromise on our relationships and on the simple joys of life because we want freedom from suffering.

When there is excessive heat, we cool our rooms and when nature declares it's going to be cold, we have room heaters. All our endeavours are geared towards avoiding unpleasant experiences and increasing pleasant ones. Yet, tragically, despite all our attempts, there are some painful events we just can't avoid, such as death, disease and old age.

NAPOLEON AND ROCKEFELLER vs. THE COMMON MAN

The Rockefellers were devastated when their 23-year-old son, Michael, who went out to Asmat near the Indonesian islands, was eaten by the cannibals there. They were among the wealthiest people in the world, yet their money couldn't prevent this tragedy.

The mighty French emperor Napoleon is a legend. His wartime strategies are taught in most military schools around the world, even 200 years after his death. He is considered one of the greatest army generals in history. Yet, after the French defeat in Waterloo, he was arrested and deported by the British to the St Helena islands in south-western Africa. While languishing there as a prisoner for six months before his eventual death, he faced harsh treatment, scorn and neglect from the soldiers.

These are just two examples, though life will offer endless such stories to tell you that material nature is unforgiving. We may discriminate between the beautiful and the ugly, the wealthy and the poor, the smart and the stupid, yet nature sees all of us as equally eligible when it comes to suffering and death.

To deal with pain and transcend the suffering associated with it, we first need humility and intelligence to recognize its all-embracing nature. No one can escape suffering, for it is an inevitable part of life. If we are unable to accept the reality of suffering, we will find life unbearable. Worry and anxiety will pursue us at every turn, and the mind will not be able to cope with the burden of daily living. Worry is likely to be the biggest killer of this millennium because the mind makes a mountain out of almost every molehill. This is typically seen in our relationships, where others never seem to meet our expectations, and we don't meet theirs. As a result, both parties are disappointed and unhappy.

CAN SCIENCE AND TECHNOLOGY HELP?

Scientific advancement helps us in many ways, it is true. For example, we have devised ways to delay old age, or to delay our acceptance of it! If your hair is turning grey, science can help you dye it. If you have too many wrinkles on your face, you can get a face lift. Losing your teeth? You can get excellent dentures. The body is inevitably ageing, and although science can't cure it, it can cover it up expertly.

Yet the solution to our problems creates a much bigger problem than the original one. Before the invention of the automobile, travel took a long time. Today, however, a journey that would have taken days in a carriage or on horseback can be done in a few hours in a motor vehicle. But now we have other problems, as you know. The automobile industry, called the 'slow bomb', has taken pollution levels to alarming heights; we lack fresh air to breathe. We had to walk long distances earlier, but now we can't breathe clean air!

Let me share a story with you. There was a saintly man who believed in peace and non-violence. As he sat in meditation under a tree, an ant from the branch above fell on his beard. As he gently tried to place the ant back on the tree, a large group of ants fell on him. In a frantic attempt to save his beard, he ran to a nearby pond and dived into it. He came out with a clean beard, but in the process of trying to save one ant, he had ended up killing so many of them.

THREE STEPS TO HANDLE SUFFERING

Suffering and pain are inevitable in this world. To recognize and accept this fact is the first step.

The second step is to see the 'intelligent' design in everything. From intercellular existence to cosmic arrangements, there is an order to everything in the cosmos. Whether it's the way the 30 trillion-plus cells work inside the body or the seasonal changes that take place, an intelligence far superior to ours is at work. All creation exists as a result of a divine intelligence; nothing exists by chance! One can then deduce how even suffering and pain in this world have some meaning – a divine plan that's far beyond our limited human intelligence to fathom. Mignon McLaughlin put it eloquently when he said, 'When suffering comes, we yearn for some sign from God, forgetting we have just had one.'

This doesn't mean we ignore our pain; it's just that we learn to accept it. If our definition of happiness is the feeling of pleasure, then all our attempts to be happy will be frustrating. This is because feelings are fleeting; they come and go. What we need in our lives is a deeper sense of purpose so we can lead truly fulfilling lives.

And that's the third and most important step: Seek what truly defines you and what it is that excites you enough to get out of bed each morning. Once you have a purpose, you can happily begin to make a difference in this world.

Yes, there will be suffering, but now your life is a complete package, full of various emotions that come and go as you live for your mission. Without a purpose, our suffering is eternal, because we live in fear. It's a life of purpose and aspiration that helps.

The next chapter teaches us how to handle failures and pain caused by the mind.

SUMMARY

- You are miserable when you get what you don't want and when you don't get what you do want.
- The three steps to cope with suffering:
  - Recognize and accept misery as inevitable.
  - See a divine plan and intelligent design in everything, from the intercellular existence to vast cosmic arrangements.
  - A deep sense of purpose – of what truly defines you – and living by that vision can help you transcend daily unhappiness and pleasures.

CHAPTER SEVEN

Accepting Failures Bravely

'The wound is the place where the light enters you.'
— Rumi

HISTORY IS REPLETE WITH examples of men and women who have braved all kinds of challenges. Most successful people today are those who have seen their share of failures and low moments.

Bollywood superstar Amitabh Bachchan is a classic example of this. Although his voice claims an iconic status today, he was once rejected by All India Radio because they didn't like his voice! He worked in 13 box-office disasters before he tasted success. And in his mid-fifties, after a series of financial debacles, he was on the verge of bankruptcy.

He faced these failures bravely, held on to life, let the bad times pass, and is a legend today. Loved by many for his willingness to learn, he has never thrown his weight around or behaved badly on film sets. Life has humbled him and he has moved on graciously.

This simply goes to show that the inner world of a successful person is as fragile as yours or mine. But the difference is that they chose to move beyond the negative chatter of their minds and instead used the mind as an ally to deal with their difficulties.

ACCEPTING RESPONSIBILITY FOR OUR SUFFERING

The Srimad Bhagavatam (11.22–23) reveals the story of a man who was extremely wealthy yet, due to his miserly nature, had made many enemies. He refused to spend money on himself and his family. Slowly, people turned against him and, suddenly, one day, he lost everything. At that moment, his family too rejected him and he faced terrible suffering. His mind was tormented by this sudden reversal of his fortunes.

People ridiculed him, threw stones at him; they passed urine on the food he got by begging, and even spat at him.

The story, however, took an amazing turn.

The man searched for answers deep within himself; he paused, chose to connect with himself and slowly realized that no one but he was to blame for his misery. He separated himself from his mind, and it soon dawned on him that it was his mind alone that caused attraction and repulsion, friends and enemies, and all the other dualities in his life.

This awareness filled his heart with peace and he instantly found shelter beyond his own mind.

The man had failed and he accepted that there was no point in blaming anyone else; he simply had to rise above his circumstances and move forward.

THE ART OF DODGING THE MIND

How do you face the surging waves in an ocean? If you turn your back towards the waves, you'll never know when a breaking wave will hit you and throw you off your feet. If you fight them, you'll be frustrated when huge waves pull you down with their immense force. The way out is to become smarter – don't fight them, don't run away from them; instead, just find a way to negotiate with them.

Stand sideways with your feet wide apart. As the waves come close, jump high or swim over them. Riding the crest will thrill you, and you'll be able to look back at your friends on the shore. And if the wave breaks in front of you, dive under the water with your arms in front. After it passes, you'll rise again to see the spectacular display back on the shore. It's fun if you can recognize the wave and either rise above it or dive below it. You can spend hours that way on the beach.

How about dodging the crazy, gushing waves of the mind, though?

While you can say no to a swim in the ocean, you have no choice when the waves of desire engulf you. You are trapped in an ocean called the mind. You can either curse your fate or seize the opportunity to blossom; you could be a rare, beautiful rose in this wild sea of turbulent emotions and stormy desires, and find a way to keep centred.

When negative thoughts fill your mind – for example, when you are plagued by thoughts that are hateful, envious or angry – it is easy to be in denial and pretend you are not carrying such thoughts. On the other hand, if your solution to negative thoughts is to merely cover them up with positive thoughts and tell yourself that life's okay and everything is fine, you are simply ignoring the undertow that will drag you deep into the ocean in no time.

You can also choose to challenge these waves and fight them, but you will be vanquished. We stand no chance against the terrible waves unleashed by the mind – until we choose to ride them.

COPING WITH THE MIND

When a spiritual practitioner faces a strong desire that is unhealthy, he doesn't seek to gratify it, nor does he hate himself for the desire. He simply rises above the 'wave' – he sees himself as separate from the mind. He lets the thought pass, even as he swims happily in his spiritual practice. If, however, the desire overwhelms his mind, he humbly surrenders to God; he bows to the Lord in his heart and escapes the lashing waves that threaten to break the backbone of his spiritual life.

You can either transcend the mind or surrender to God. Both these acts help us not only escape the mind's forces but also enjoy life more fully. This how a spiritual practitioner tackles the challenges posed by the mind. When desires come, one does not worry, for one knows that the flood of desires shall soon pass.

When you are in such a place, I would tell you not to panic, fret or fume. Gently manoeuvre the situation; pray, call a friend or simply pause and breathe. The tidal waves of desires are here to stay. When one passes, another is round the corner. Don't waste time fighting them. Learn to live with them without surrendering to the yearnings. Let's not give the mind and its untold madness any more importance than it deserves.

DON'T PANIC; HANG AROUND

The cart procession in the coastal town of Jagannath, in Puri, can be scary for the weak-hearted. Over 1.2 million people attend the annual 2-km procession.

The gigantic carts rattle along the Grand Road, pulled by hundreds of men and women, both young and old, while thousands try to get close to the rope to touch it. The massive wheels of the cart move with a crackling sound, while men in the cart beat their drums in a rhythmic metre. It's an imposing sight that heralds the arrival of the Lord of the Universe.

For those who prefer to watch the parade from the side, it's a challenge. As the cart comes closer, many push towards the edge of the road, seeking the pavement's shelter, which is already bursting with people. Two types of people get hurt in the frenzy. One lot consists of those rushing away from the cart to the apparent safety of the pavement, not realizing that they will get caught in the stampede there. The other lot are those who push and fight the crowd to join in the pulling, and many of them get injured in that mass of bodies.

What's the safest position? Just stay where you are; gently bend and move sideways. Let the pandemonium pass. If you overcome your fear of the crowd and resist the urge to escape, you'll find a place for yourself right in the middle of the chaos. You'll remain peaceful even as people around you panic or scream in passion.

Srila Prabhupada gave a one-word solution to tackle the crazy whims of the mind: neglect. The mind will scream and protest. Don't panic, don't fear and resist the urge to escape. You will surely discover peace in the madness of this world.

Now, you may wonder what it means to 'neglect' the mind and how one can do that when life cause us so much pain and suffering. In the next two chapters, we shall explore the psychology of blame games and see how we can take responsibility for our suffering.

SUMMARY

- While swimming in an ocean, we don't fight or show our back to the waves; we simply jump high or dive under with our arms stretched out in front of us. Similarly, when the waves of desire strike, a spiritual practitioner either rises above them or bows to the Lord in prayer.
- Two examples are given to show the following:
  - The inner world of most successful people is as fragile as ours, yet they succeed because they choose to be stronger than the dictates of the mind.
  - Misery is universal, and our heroism lies not in external success but in how we face our suffering.
  - To live with integrity and principles even when challenged by injustice speaks of a high character.
- The Srimad Bhagavatam teaches us that if we search deep within, we'll discover the real cause of our misery – the mind. This awareness can fill the heart with peace and provide a sense of shelter that is far richer than what the mind can offer.

CHAPTER EIGHT

Do You Blame Others for Your Emotional Pain?

'My dear Lord, one who patiently waits for your blessings during suffering, and offers respects with his heart, words and body, has liberation as his rightful claim.'
– Srimad Bhagavatam (10.14.8)

TWO-YEAR-OLD HEER was inconsolable. Her parents, uncles, grandfather, older sister and my friend Manish tried their best to appease the child. She wailed and wailed, taking in deep shuddering breaths between her cries.

It was now the father's turn to quieten the baby. With his left arm, he picked her up and with his right, he began hitting the small study desk from which the girl had fallen. Pointing to the table, the father indulged his baby. 'You terrible table! How dare you hurt our lovely diamond, Heer?' He then took the child's fragile hands and helped her slap the board's surface. He chastised the board. 'Here. Take this for making our darling cry.' As everyone mollycoddled little Heer, she seemed satisfied and soon stopped crying. The elders continued their conversation, while the baby got busy with something else.

Manish came up to me and whispered, 'Do you realize they pretend as if nothing has happened, while they have just been violent to their child?'

'What are you saying?' I asked, surprised. 'I thought they loved her and gave the poor thing all the attention she needed.'

'Did you notice they taught little Heer that the table was responsible for her fall? That damned table is guilty!'

'So what?' I said dismissively. 'That's a harmless way to pacify a child.'

Manish's eyes widened. 'No, my friend, it's dreadful. The child has learnt a bad lesson today – that others cause her pain. Later in life, when she goes through emotional pain, she'll quickly look for a table to hit. Our elders teach us the blame game early on in life. We are taught that we are not responsible for our happiness; others, like the desk in this instance, cause us pain and suffering. It's a harmful message that we have all internalized.'

COPING WITH PAIN

If your loved one rejects you on a day when it rained heavily, chances are that a downpour on another day will trigger that memory of rejection. The echoes of emotional pain are felt for a long period of time. With poor self-care habits, even a minor issue could nag you for months, and even a small trigger could cause havoc inside you.

When someone hates you and judges your intentions wrongly, the hurt can be worse than the pain of broken limbs. If you slip and fall while walking, even strangers may help you get up; they seem to understand your predicament. But if you are taunted or humiliated by your boss, and you are deeply hurt, even your best friends may not fully realize what you are going through. People may empathize with your physical suffering, but rarely do they know about your emotional struggles.

We often hear of people who committed suicide because a lover rejected them. What does this prove? Emotional trauma is more intense than physical suffering. While medicines can remove, or at least camouflage, bodily pain, emotional wounds can increase with time and hence require a different approach.

Since the triggers and associations of emotional pain are many, the least we can do is stop blaming others for our misery. Instead, let's choose more humane and sensitive techniques for our inner world.

PLAYING THE BLAME GAME

The common mistake most people commit when they are emotionally troubled is to hover at one of two extremes: they either hold others guilty for their misery or indulge in self-pity. We lose the ability to objectively see the suffering for what it is.

Blame ensures that we look for external reasons for our frustrations and thereby escape responsibility for ourselves and what we are feeling. Even if you convince another person that he is the cause of your suffering, can you change your unhappy state within? No. Sadly, most people are caught playing the blame game. It's when you pull up your socks and take responsibility for your own happiness that you stand a chance to transform your miserable state into a more peaceful existence.

The first time we accept the lie of another's guilt, we may be conscious of what we have done, but soon, our very being integrates with the tales we tell ourselves. When my falsehood becomes an unshakeable belief, I need no enemies because I have successfully destroyed myself.

What do we do now?

MOVING FROM BLAME TO GROWTH

What if you are a victim of abuse? Shouldn't the wrongdoer be blamed here? Of course, you should report the crime and seek support. And if you are going through post-traumatic stress disorder (PTSD), you need immediate treatment. But the principle is to focus on caring for yourself rather than to blame others. We have to do what it takes to nurture and protect the physical self, but we also need to take care of our emotional well-being. While we bring the perpetrators of violent abuse to book and fight against injustice, we also need to shift our focus within to find solutions for our emotional well-being.

An effective way to reconnect with your natural and happy state is by substituting blame with the intention to grow. For example, let's say you lose your job. What you shouldn't do is brood over your boss's vindictive nature or your mistakes, if you had made any.

At the same time, see what you can do better the next time you are in a similar situation. For this, you can use the tool of visualization. This tool can quickly transform a negative loop into a virtuous cycle of definite possibility.

One day, during a light-hearted conversation with Rajesh, my old, saintly and joyful ashram friend, I was surprised by his confession: he was unable to forgive his senior leader for insulting him in front of over a hundred people. I was shocked when I discovered that the incident had happened over 15 years earlier, during a day-long seminar. I realized that the scolding still haunted him and he often fantasized about revenge. His beatific smiles were misleading; behind his cheerful exterior, he was angry and full of shame. He needed help.

I asked him what positive things he could do if the event were to happen again. We discussed a few possibilities, like humbly protesting at the time or quietly leaving the hall as a mark of disapproval; he could even confront his superior two days later and express how the insult had hurt him. Between the two of us, we replayed the event where he did what we had agreed on was the acceptable and positive thing to do. He confessed that he now felt empowered. He was able to change the course of his future, because he had exercised control over his present choice of thoughts and actions.

EMBRACE FREEDOM

Blaming others is tempting because it helps us avoid taking charge of our situation and seems to absolve us of guilt. This has its share of deadly consequences. We drift away from the truth and thereby intensify our emotional pain. The fact is that the present moment is *your* reality, and nobody can take it away from you. And all of your past mistakes and tragedies cannot undermine your future. It's the 'now' that you can control. The more you take charge of your life, the more likely you are to feel more empowered and peaceful.

Blaming others is an iron shackle that heavily curtails *your* freedom. Let's, therefore, choose to accept what has happened and make the right choice now, of living a blameless and responsible life! The reality is that it is responsibility, not blame, that brings emotional freedom.

If you are worried not about blaming others, but about dealing with the negativity and hate coming from others, Chapter 9 teaches you how to face haters.

SUMMARY

- We learn to blame others early on in our life. For example, when a child falls from a cradle, the elders blame the floor.
- Blaming others and self-pity are two extremes of emotional weakness.
- The solution is:
  - taking responsibility for your suffering;
  - exploring lessons to learn; and
  - visualizing a different response to the same provocation.

CHAPTER NINE

Dealing with Hate

'O Arjuna, all beings are born to delusion and duality – thus desire and hate drives them.'

– Bhagavad Gita (7.27)

MY STOMACH WRITHED IN pain but I was aware that this was not a physical ache. He stood up suddenly and yelled in the middle of the meeting, 'You are a bunch of eunuchs, good for nothing, just whiling your time away, never productive.' I was totally gutted. My head exploded with a hundred possible ways to return the fire. But what I saw next left me stunned.

Aki, my boss and the intended victim of the outburst, adjusted his glasses and smiled at the slanderer. After a pause, in the pin-drop silence, he said softly but clearly, 'Now that you have raised sufficient doubts on our gender, we need to do our homework and get back to you by the next meeting.' His disarming comment eased the tension in the room, and a few other members laughed nervously. The man's tirade was cut short. He sat down abruptly. I had never witnessed something like this in my life. Here, a blatant insult had been diffused in the most unusual way by the chairperson of the committee.

RECOGNIZE THE CHILD WITHIN

At that time, I had just begun my secretarial services and was floored by the display of charm and ready wit by my boss, even under a highly provocative situation. I then started to associate myself more closely with Aki, to grow and learn from him.

One day, I asked him the secret to his calm disposition. I wondered how he internally resolves the unreasonable and malicious statements his detractors sometimes throw at him. He said matter-of-factly, 'I take their feedback seriously, but not their behaviour or the rulings on my character.'

Referring to the recent attack on his effectiveness, the one I had been witness to, Aki sighed. 'Learn to see them – especially when they lose it – as children. If a child misbehaves, we don't judge them, we don't see any mean intention behind their actions. The child must be hungry or hasn't got enough sleep, we reason. Well, children do grow up, but I know there's still a 'child' within them who can behave badly. Adults, like this man who insulted me, have enough worries in life; maybe they too are victims of their circumstances. I give them the benefit of the doubt.'

'That's generous of you,' I replied. 'I mean, I could never do it.'

'Yes, to see others empathically, we need to see ourselves with care and compassion.'

I was intrigued.

Aki continued. 'If we inherently hate ourselves and lack self-respect, we transfer our "badness" to others because that's our familiar environment; unfortunately, to dislike and disrespect is natural to us, and we do that with ourselves and with others. Besides, if we tell ourselves sad stories, we attract similar situations. Therefore, the golden rule of emotional hygiene is to be kind to yourself and trust yourself. Then learn to see others with compassion.'

The lesson I learnt from Aki that evening is that there's an inner child within each one of us, and for so long, we've either neglected or hurt our inner child. Now it's time to love it, and this is called self-love.

SELF-ACCEPTANCE

You tend to deal with those who dislike you, or continuously criticize you, for no sound reason by avoiding them. But if you can't dodge their missiles, then your strongest arsenal is self-belief and self-acceptance. If you also hate yourself, then negative behaviour from others will only intensify your suffering. So you need to like yourself first. And stay emotionally strong by surrounding yourself with good friends and well-wishers, who bring meaning to your life.

With this strength, you can then learn to ignore your detractors internally and even learn to forgive them or see them as victims of insecurity, fear, anger or similar emotions. Hermann Hesse said, 'If you hate a person, you hate something in him that is part of yourself. What isn't part of ourselves doesn't disturb us.'

Often when people detest you, it's because of who they are, not because of who you are. This kind of thinking is a critical first step for self-preservation in a world that regularly throws strange and unpleasant surprises at us. With so much uncertainty around us, we need to depend on ourselves, and we must keep our own thoughts, feelings and beliefs under control.

Thus, tell yourself that who you are is independent of anyone else's judgement of you and whether they love you or despise you.

FROM 'GRIEF' TO 'GRACE'

Once when I was still working with Aki, an acquaintance spewed venom at me in a WhatsApp group. He accused me, apart from questioning my moral scruples, of playing 'politics'. A certain management decision that I was part of had irked him. I was bewildered, and it showed on my face.

Aki saw me the next morning and suggested I move from a space of hurt or grief to kindness or grace. His suggestion was simple, but effective: 'Close your eyes, breathe slowly and deeply as you send goodness, love or warmth to your critic.' I did feel some relief on doing so, and Aki clarified that this was a practical step in moving towards compassion and forgiveness.

He then asked me what I loved to do. I used to learn verses from the scriptures as a hobby, and he suggested I do that right away. Not only did that distract me from the hate-filled message, but it also helped me discover my inner peace – after all, I was not used to people lashing out at me. Aki smiled mischievously. 'Welcome, son, you are now baptized in the world of management.' He then paraphrased a quote by a wise man: 'Criticism is something you can easily avoid if you say nothing, do nothing and be nothing.' Over time, I realized that the gentleman who despised me had problems with others as well, and when I shared this with Aki, he jested, 'If Aki has a problem with everyone, then Aki is the problem.'

When people pass critical judgements against you, it usually stems from their own insecurities. They, unfortunately, try to feel better by throwing their inner negativity at those around them. If someone has a piece of stinking fish stuck to his moustache, he'll likely declare that the whole world smells. Aki warned me, 'If you too hate him, remember now it's both of you suffering. You can't drink poison and expect *him* to die!'

LESSONS FROM THE SRIMAD BHAGAVATAM

The Srimad Bhagavatam begins with the episode of a bull that resisted the urge to hate. Religion was personified as a bull, his legs broken by Kali, the personification of evil. The perpetrator of this cruelty was evident to anyone who saw the incident, especially to Parikshit, the emperor, who was ready to punish Kali. Still, Religion refused to play the blame game and forgave Kali.

In stark contrast, there is another episode in the Gita where Daksha's insinuations and scorn only make matters worse. Daksha abused Lord Shiva, and Shiva's followers retaliated; the situation spun out of control as violence, suicide and gruesome murders followed in rapid succession. When we counter hatred with more hate, it's what Martin Luther King Jr said about driving darkness away with more darkness – and, in this case, it was more like using an AK-47 assault rifle to get rid of a mosquito.

The most dramatic episode of restraint and respect in the Gita – the one that reminds me of Aki's response to the angry man – is seen when the sage Durvasa attempted to kill the Lord's devotee King Ambarish for breaking his fast without waiting for him. Known and feared widely for his temper tantrums, Durvasa went berserk as he created a huge monster to kill Ambarish for what was, in fact, a trivial matter. Lord Vishnu came to His devotee's rescue by immediately discharging his fiery disc, which not only destroyed the demon but chased the sage around the Universe. Fearing for his life, Durvasa at last realized his folly and begged for forgiveness from the king, who patiently waited for over a year to welcome his guest back. The king not only forgave him, but took care of the sage by appeasing his hunger.

The world needs more Ambarishs and Akis to teach us to forgive, live, let live and love during our brief sojourn in this world.

You may feel that you too have a need to feel loved and be forgiven. How can you improve your chances of getting love from yourself as well as from others in this world? Appreciation is the answer, and Chapter 10 elaborates on this principle.

SUMMARY

- When people behave badly towards us, it's usually because the 'child' within them is disturbed.
- The golden rule of emotional hygiene is to be kind to yourself and treat others with compassion.
- When people hate you, to prevent your mind from troubling you, you can do three things:
  - Practise self-belief and surround yourself with friends who trust you and love you.
  - Send 'love', 'warmth' or 'grace' to your critic.
  - Absorb yourself in activities that define you and give you a sense of worth.

CHAPTER TEN

The Wonder of Appreciation

'If one offers Me with love and devotion a leaf, a flower, a fruit or water, I will accept it.'

– Bhagavad Gita (9.26)

HOW DO YOU FEEL when you have really worked hard on something and nobody acknowledges it, leave alone appreciates you for the service? Just as you are feeling low and lost, somebody comes along, recognizes what you have done and admires your sincerity. At that moment, what's the feeling inside you? Do you feel valued, encouraged, worthy and inspired to serve more?

SEEING THE GOOD IN SMALL THINGS

This just reveals how powerful appreciation is. You can make an enormous investment in a relationship by simply offering encouraging words. And it costs you nothing. Plus, it doesn't have to be for something spectacular. Once, a friend appreciated the way I ate lunch – silently, with grace. He said I chewed each morsel as if it was an act of meditation. I felt good and worthy, although I hadn't done much good to others by eating my own food. One thing became clear to me then; small, truthful, kind words spread goodness immediately.

Once a person challenged me, saying that we make friends only if we flatter and when we speak the truth, we only make enemies. I politely disagreed; we can see the 'truth' even in the small things that people do and then acknowledge and appreciate them fully. The gains are tremendous – heartfelt blessings from the other person. If we can resolve to appreciate and thank at least three to five people every day for what they are doing or who they are, we'll be amazed by the goodness that we earn in return.

HOW IS APPRECIATION DIFFERENT FROM FLATTERY?

Flattery is an insincere technique to manipulate others. Appreciation, on the other hand, is truthful and warm; it's a universal principle that spreads goodness and love, within and without. Studies have shown that the greatest emotional need of a human being is to feel appreciated. And, paradoxically, when we offer this gift to others, we receive abundantly from the Universe. Unlike money, which you will have less of if you give it away, giving appreciation makes you as emotionally rich as the person receiving your thanks.

A LESSON FROM A TAXI DRIVER

I learnt this lesson when, after an unpleasant management meeting at the ashram, I had to use a taxi. I was disturbed and angry, and the ride that day, which usually takes half an hour, took longer. I tried to relax but found it difficult due to my agitated state.

I noticed the roads were overcrowded with cars honking and pedestrians crossing with utter disregard to traffic rules. However, my driver was sensitive and did not honk at other vehicles. I was surprised to see him patiently navigating the traffic. After we reached my destination, I paused to thank him for his considerate driving. I also confessed that I was disturbed and that his quiet tolerance of other vehicles helped me reorganize myself mentally. He was elated. He profusely thanked me for appreciating him and then made a candid confession in turn. When he had begun driving the car, he had seen me in his rear-view mirror and noticed I was piqued about something. He consciously chose to please me and was glad that it had helped me. I felt touched and thanked him again. And, magically, I felt all my frustrations evaporate.

Offering and receiving kindness had a profound effect on my consciousness. The rest of the day passed smoothly.

Later, I reflected that if a positive exchange with a stranger made me so happy, what incredible treasures awaited me if I made kindness a regular practice with people who matter to me? If we allow thankfulness to be a one-off experience, our lives won't change much, because the tempest of negativity and cynicism, which is the reality of this world, will swallow us. We need to consistently choose to appreciate, and only then will we have control over our lives.

We also need to remember that appreciation is not an isolated practice. We have to integrate it with patience and fortitude: patience to hold on till God reciprocates, and heroic courage to face criticism or a lack of reciprocation from others. But if we are sincere, everything will soon fall into place; the world is an echo and we eventually get back what we give.

WHY WE DON'T GET APPRECIATION FROM OTHERS

Unfortunately, many live in the space of gossip and assumptions. The Universe then reduces their chances of getting appreciation from others as well. Gossip is the other side of the coin of flattery; it's what we say behind someone's back that we wouldn't say to their face. Flattery, on the other hand, is what we'd say to their face that we wouldn't say behind their back!

We make wrong assumptions due to four defects in us. Firstly, we have imperfect senses and, as a result, fall into the trap of illusions. When we fall into this trap, we make mistakes and, to cover up these errors, we cheat. For example, if you have an orange after tasting a lemon, it may taste sweet. But after eating a cup of sugar, the same orange will taste sour. Based on this illusion, created due to our imperfect senses, one may decide to abandon the orange and then also justify his action to others or wrongly criticize the orange for being sour.

The Srimad Bhagavatam reveals the plight of Hiranyakashipu, who assumed he was immortal. He received a boon that would allow him to remain invincible during the day and night, and not get killed by a human or an animal, either by hand or by a weapon. He also acquired the benediction that he wouldn't die inside the house or outside it, and neither on land nor in the sky. At one time, Hiranyakashipu was the most powerful man on this planet; by merely moving his eyebrows, he could command the sun to rise or set.

He thought he had smartly conquered death, but Time humbled him when the Lord assumed the form of Narasimha, neither animal nor human, and killed him. If his assumptions about his glory and power were crushed to dust, what's the fate of our weak assumptions?

The Ramayana tell us that Vibhishana was the younger brother of Ravana, but he chose to abandon him and join the virtuous Rama instead. However, Rama's dutiful servants, led by Sugriva, wrongly assumed that Vibhishana was like his brother and, therefore, couldn't be trusted. Finally, Rama revealed Vibhishana's character and also accepted him as his friend. Vibhishana went on to play a critical role in the victory of Rama over Ravana. Had the warriors on Rama's side decided to reject Vibhishana, the Ramayana may have taken a different course.

I saw the deadly effect of criticism and wrong assumptions when, on a 36-hour train journey, I met Anand, an acquaintance from our community. Although we had interacted briefly earlier, I had heard a lot of negative things about him and his family. During the course of our travel, however, we spoke at length and got to know each other better.

I soon realized he was exactly the opposite of what I had assumed about him. He was helpful, hardworking and grateful to the community members, and not lazy or selfish as I had thought him to be. I was inspired by his association and, by the time we reached our destination, I had earned an excellent friend for life. At the same time, I also felt ashamed for having misjudged him. I learnt a valuable lesson that day: don't make wrong assumptions about others based on hearsay. Instead, give them the benefit of the doubt.

How often we wrongly judge people based on scanty evidence. We instantly assume somebody is a crook if he's from a particular community or believe things about someone's character based on the colour of his skin. The result? We relish harmful thinking and it becomes addictive. This is poisonous because it feeds on itself. We become compulsive rumour-mongers. Eventually, we are totally disconnected from ourselves – our higher, virtuous nature.

It's little wonder then that many end up betraying their own values, and consequently feel unloved and unfulfilled.

WHY DO WE CRITICIZE?

We spread rumours and judge wrongly because of a deep need within us to feel good about ourselves. Unfortunately, this strategy is poor because we derive, or try to derive, our self-worth from the failure of others. When we speak ill of others, we subtly imagine that we are better than others in some way or another. We are actually seeking self-approval, but because we approach it in the wrong manner, we go further away from our true selves.

Tearing a person down or passing negative and irresponsible comments about others can also subtly make us feel guilty when that person is in front of us. Even if we are desensitized from guilt, the act never goes unpardoned; it comes back in some form to haunt us. Basically, we'll never be happy if it's in our nature to see faults in others.

The solution is simple: Seek self-approval through healthy means and don't speak harshly about anyone. Be kind and compassionate to others.

COURAGE TO ASK QUESTIONS AND
CHANGE OUR ASSUMPTIONS

Imagine the person you are tempted to speak negatively about is present with you in the conversation. Would you then speak about him or her in the same way? If yes, then go ahead and say what you want to say. It's okay to be critical, but if you wouldn't say it in their presence, then don't say it in their absence.

The strength to resist gossip and challenge our assumptions requires courage and humility. And there is no way we can circumvent these sacred principles and still have healthy relationships with ourselves and with others.

Maharaj Parikshit was on a hunting expedition. He got tired and thirsty, and approached a hermitage for shelter. However, the ashram's sage was in a meditative trance and did not extend hospitality to the king, who assumed that the sage was simply pretending to meditate. Angry, the king garlanded the sage with a dead snake and left in a huff.

Soon, however, he discovered his assumption about the great sage was wrong, and that he had made a mistake. He went back to apologize for his actions. The sage's young son, not acknowledging the repentant king, assumed in turn that the king was haughty. The boy declared that the king deserved to die, and cursed him. Parikshit showed his real character and passed the test by cheerfully welcoming the curse, saying he deserved it for having offended a pure sage.

It's interesting to note that although the king had made wrong assumptions in the first place, his internal humility to accept his mistake makes him a heroic character in Vedic history. The king was righteous and always protected his citizens. He had even seen God when he was just in his mother's womb, and always made the right decisions. If powerful men can make incorrect assumptions, how can lesser individuals not do the same?

What we need to do is to ask questions. But because we lack the courage to ask, we assume. And then we replace communication with rumour-mongering and assumptions. The wily mind can then cause immense damage. It is only humility that can save us from the trap the ego and the mind lay for us.

LEARNING TO APPRECIATE ONESELF

I have had people say to me: 'I always appreciate others, but no one encourages me. I am only giving. I too need love.'

In that case, you can learn to appreciate yourself as well.

Once, during a workshop with a group of monks, I sensed a feeling of inadequacy and self-doubt among some members. I gave them an exercise where participants seated in pairs were asked to share something they really appreciated about themselves. An uneasy silence filled the room. One of them said he would rather not do the exercise because he wasn't comfortable appreciating his own self; he'd rather appreciate others. I left him alone, and the others reluctantly began the exercise.

Soon, the energy levels in the room changed; it was as if a mass of thick dark clouds had made way for bright sunshine. There were smiles and happy exchanges; it was obvious that they were enjoying the exercise. The one who refused to do the exercise looked anxious; he asked me if he could do the exercise too now. I partnered him up with another monk and heard him talk about the qualities he was grateful for. It wasn't easy for him; he'd often slip into talking about his own follies and limitations instead. After some prompting by me, he ended up doing the exercise fairly well.

Later, he confessed that he felt refreshed by the experience. Yet, a strange fear gripped him: 'Maybe I am haughty for thinking so highly of myself.' I explained to him that he was used to following an inner script where hate for himself was normal. His eyes lit up and he exclaimed, 'Yes, that's my problem.'

Many secretly despise themselves. They hate the way they look, they condemn themselves for what they have done all their lives and they refuse to acknowledge any good they have done. As a result, they are unable to appreciate others fully. Even if they do, it comes across as inauthentic. To be able to appreciate others, we need to feel worthy and appreciate the beautiful creation that is the individual self. You are the most unique person in the world. It's time you learnt to celebrate this gift quietly with gratitude.

The challenge for many is that when they make mistakes it seems like the end of the world to them. One mantra I heard long ago that helps me when I catch myself indulging in self-loathing acts is: *I may have made many mistakes, but I am not a mistake*. It's time we appreciate God's gift to us – our abilities and our own uniqueness.

How can we ensure we love ourselves and yet stay grounded? Chapter 11 offers a solution and, more importantly, reassures us that self-love is not the antithesis of humility.

SUMMARY

- Seeing good in small things and a fulsome appreciation of the same attracts positive energy.
- We don't receive appreciation because we usually live in a space of gossip and assumptions.
- We make wrong assumptions because of four defects:
  - our imperfect senses;
  - our tendency to fall into the trap of illusions;
  - our propensity to make mistakes; and
  - cheating.
- Two qualities help us check our assumptions regularly: humility and courage. Asking questions is the simple way to check our assumptions.
- We spread rumours because we have chosen a poor strategy for improving our self-worth: we try and derive our success from the failures of others. Instead, we can begin to seek self-approval in a healthy way.
- Those who hate themselves are unable to give appreciation.
- Offer a sincere appreciation of yourself and celebrate your individuality.

CHAPTER ELEVEN

Is Self-love Safe and Healthy?

'My dear Krishna, Your Lordship has protected us from a poisoned cake, from a great fire, from cannibals, from the vicious assembly, from sufferings during our exile in the forest and from the battle where great generals fought. And now You have saved us from the weapon of Ashwatthama.'
— Kunti's prayers in Srimad Bhagavatam (1.8.24)

'I NEED HONEST FEEDBACK because I want to improve,' a young monk told our community members after his first class. I frankly pointed out his mistakes to him. Later, I heard from a friend that he was upset at my sharp observations. But he asked for it, I thought. However, I soon understood that his desire for feedback actually veiled, for behind those words was actually a need to be loved.

How often we have all felt a need to be wanted and accepted by others, which we then seek in social interactions. But when this doesn't happen, we feel let down. If you find yourself in such a situation very often, it means that you are someone who lets others decide your happiness and self-worth.

The solution is simple: love and accept yourself; seek validation from your own heart.

You might wonder if self-love is healthy. After all, for millennia, hubris has trapped men. How often we see men overrate their abilities so much so that they lose touch with reality. I have often been challenged: will self-love lead to over-the-top self-confidence? Further, most religious traditions cite examples of saints who loathed their own existence. Their prayers reveal deep lamentation, and many preachers encourage us to meditate on our own inadequacies.

I generally respond to these fears with a counter-question: Can you criticize yourself without becoming depressed? What's the guarantee that if you reflect on your failings, you won't slip into hopelessness, which is simply another side of the hubris coin? Isn't that also a case of ego obsession, about how 'I' am bad? You will see that 'I' remains the centre here as well.

A simple way to love your own self and yet not be a victim of false pride is by having the safety net of 'Fresh Gratitude'.

FRESH GRATITUDE: THE ANTIDOTE FOR FALSE PRIDE

Being in gratitude is a deeply empowering act. To practise this attitude all the time, no matter what occurs in life, helps you remain centred and calm in the face of life's ups and downs. So it is a wonderful way to deal with the suffering life brings.

Further, gratitude also helps prevent a sense of false pride, and actually allows you to love and respect yourself and others, as well as accept everything that life brings you. When you are truly in gratitude for yourself and your life, you are able to love and appreciate yourself truly. This is what I would call healthy self-love as opposed to pride or ego.

Thanking our parents, God, family and friends on a daily basis is very beneficial. But along with that, we could also send thanks for the events and blessings we have received each day. When we do this, our gratitude practice is realistic and also relevant to each day and what it brings. This helps keep the practice fresh and new each day.

You constantly look out for things to be thankful for. It could be a lovely breakfast, a good workout at your gym or a catchy song that you hear one day. It could be anything at all, and if you sincerely send thanks for what you have received, you have tapped into the gift of gratitude. The result is that you will be humble and come to feel deep within that the Universe is benevolent and loving.

American linguist S.I. Hayakawa created a concept called the 'Ladder of Abstraction' that describes the way humans think and communicate in varying degrees of abstraction. At the bottom of this ladder are concrete things, like a five-bedroom house, a red Mercedez Benz or a thin-crust pizza topped with olives and jalapeños. At the top of the ladder are the abstract ideas of those things, that is, the concept of residence, vehicle or food respectively.

Many are stuck either at the top or the bottom of this ladder. For example, one person might be so busy with his daily worries that he has no time to appreciate the Universe, God and his own existence in this giant cosmos. On the other hand, another might speak vaguely about God's love and how we need to transcend the world and its problems; he could be so caught in lofty principles that he forgets to pay his bills or buy groceries.

An evolved person, however, is one who moves up and down this ladder gracefully; he understands God's love through specific gratitude techniques. Gratitude can be practised at both the top and the bottom of this ladder. At the lowest rung, we can thank the Universe for its daily gifts. At a more abstract level, we could connect to the Universe and our place in it. The thankfulness expressed for our belonging in the Universe here helps us experience a world above this one.

I knew two monks who, at different times, decided to get married after living in the monastery for over 15 years. One of them struggled in his marriage because he would only discuss and do specific things in his married life. His wife complained that he just couldn't relax or talk without an agenda. The poor man had been a manager his whole life – he had lived at the bottom of the ladder; he didn't relish spontaneity or ambiguous discussions. The other monk faced problems due to his vague dependence on God. His wife would want him to address specific issues, but he'd say God would take care of them. This man was trapped at the top of the ladder!

IS SELF-CONDEMNATION HEALTHY?

Some people think we should constantly criticize ourselves – like the holy saints of the past – and that by doing so, we attract God's grace. But for a person who carries the heavy baggage of emotional trauma, it's more practical to attract God's blessings by thanking Him rather than by condemning oneself. Moreover, the saints of the past didn't contrive self-criticism or humility; it just flowed naturally from their souls. They didn't have to 'try' and feel lowly; it just happened because they felt God's love and therefore everything else that belonged to this world, including their own existence, paled in comparison. It's the overwhelming experience of devotion – 'effective' devotion, not 'executive' devotion that explains the humility of advanced spiritual practitioners. They didn't practise feeling fallen. Unfortunately, many who imitate these great souls end up feeling depressed because it is not spontaneous.

A heart that is not experiencing rich love cannot criticize itself. And if we consciously engage in self-condemnation, we simply attract lower energies. It's better to appreciate the self, thank God and then allow the heart to be filled with God's love. Over time, this practice will lead one to spontaneously apologize for her inadequacies.

If you are already miserable, don't make your condition worse by giving undue importance to the vicious critic in your head. Self-criticism helps only if you learn and grow from it. To live successfully with yourself, what you really need is self-acceptance. And to sustain your relationships with others, you need a healthy habit of self-criticism, in that it is healthy to look at your mistakes objectively. But it is more important to live faithfully. Then you won't need approval from others because your external life will be consistent with your inner values.

Learn to celebrate God's gift of this one blessed life you have. And if you find that difficult, you could be thankful for the fact that you can read and write this essay, or have a good digestion allowing you to eat your food, or have eyes that let you see the world. Just start somewhere and observe the difference it makes in your life.

Do you thank God for all the gifts he has given you, but also compare yourself with others and get miserable? Chapter 12 shares tools to practise humility and maintain sanity in this world.

SUMMARY

- Instead of letting others decide our worth, we can seek validation from our own heart through self-love.
- To prevent self-love from resulting in arrogance, we need to constantly practise gratitude and appreciate others.
- To make gratitude a fresh experience and a practical concept, we could thank at least five things or people daily for the gifts we received in the past 24 hours.
- Hayakawa's 'Ladder of Abstraction' teaches us the need to gracefully move up and down from principles to specific gratitude practices.

CHAPTER TWELVE

Sanity in an Age of Intensity

'A person who is not disturbed by the incessant flow of desires—that enter like rivers into the ocean, which is ever being filled but is always still—can alone achieve peace, and not the man who strives to satisfy such desires.'

– Bhagavad Gita (2.70)

WALKING UP TOWARDS VASUDHARA Falls and Lakshmi Van in the Himalayan region of Badrinath, I got tired within the first kilometre. I was tempted to take a break when my friend Jay offered sagacious advice, 'Remember the three principles of trekking in this terrain, and it can help you march on happily even in your busy Mumbai life.'

Jay offered me these gems:

1. Stride at your natural speed and don't hurry.
2. Don't compare with others; look only at yourself.
3. Keep hiking/moving; don't stop.

Over the last decade, these simple, yet profound rules have served as a beacon of light and have often helped me out of stressful situations.

I had violated each of the rules and had fatigued myself that day. Now, I began my second innings, first by connecting with my own ordinary pace, which was independent of what I desired or how I fared on a better day. Nothing mattered except that I liaise with myself, now and here. As I renewed my climb, I let go of the urge to race against the others in our group. I repeatedly approved of myself as I was, and reminded myself that I was unique and was doing just right. And since I was moving at my regular speed, I could resist the urge to take a break. Gradually, I even lost the desire to halt.

After six hours, when I reached my destination, I was amazed to discover I was second in a group of 60! I realized I had excelled because I didn't worry about what the others were doing and instead chose to listen to my body.

These rules helped me cultivate the habit of writing and exercising daily. I repeatedly failed in these areas because I wanted to achieve too many things too soon. I was keen to see what others were doing, ostensibly for inspiration, but in reality, I was comparing myself to them, which made my life miserable. I began with the enthusiasm of a champion writer or a health freak, and in no time, the zest fizzled out. And with that, I also lost my self-confidence and belief.

After my return to Mumbai, I began the slow and steady 'Himalayan' practice Jay had taught me. I wrote and exercised much more. What others did in the gym didn't affect me. How many books my friends wrote was of no concern to me any more. And as I penned my thoughts daily, I realized that I had plenty of stuff to write about! I was rich in content as well as in health.

I had inadvertently changed the focus from the destination to the journey. So my new happiness in life was not in finishing the activity, but in doing it.

And all this happened because I chose to be me and not my idea of what others thought about me.

We often hear quotes like: 'You achieve success when you work hard for it. It doesn't fall into your lap; you can't sit idly and hope to receive it!'

So, I was surprised when, as an apprentice in our ashram two decades ago, I heard Jay say, 'Real success is dependent on how you "receive" life, not how you "achieve" it.' And in the Himalayas, Jay taught me to 'receive' – to connect with myself, rather than try to be what I was not.

Since then, my own practices and observations have convinced me of this principle.

THE PRICE OF INTENSITY

Recently, another friend declared, 'It doesn't matter what you do, but you must be passionate about it.' He spoke animatedly, 'You could be a monk or the CEO of a multinational company or even a sweeper on the street, but you must live a life of intensity.'

I politely probed, 'Why should anyone be obsessive about his profession? I am quite happy and peaceful and don't see a reason to psych myself about my profession.'

'No, you don't understand,' he said. 'This world is a battlefield; the go-getters are out to grab everything. You need to be on your toes and fight many enemies, both within and without, to be able to survive.'

'But there is no war,' I said slowly and softly. 'There is enough for everyone. Let's live and let live.'

My response shook him.

After a pause, he jabbered on, 'Er…uh…I'm sure you'll agree – after all, you are a monk – that there are many enemies in our own minds we need to fight and conquer.'

I said, 'If you think you are always fighting a war, you are simply destroying your own life.'

He looked at me sceptically.

I said, 'Intensity demands a heavy price. Your sympathetic nervous system gets overworked because a constant fight, flight and fright existence has a catabolic effect on your health. It breaks down your tissues and exhausts you. Please learn to relax and sleep well. Enjoy your work and be happy. It's all right if you are not the CEO. Do your best, and all good things will come your way.'

How each one of us responds to our environment is determined by the way the autonomic nervous system (ANS) is developed. The ANS controls all automatic actions in the body like the heart rate or digestion, which function even without your conscious control over them. There are two sections within the ANS: the sympathetic nervous system (SNS) and the parasympathetic nervous system (PSNS).

The SNS helps the body when we are stressed, because it helps us with a 'fight or flight' response during danger. Nature, however, has created a beautiful balance with the PSNS, which is anabolic and helps us rejuvenate after our 'fight or flight' experience. It helps us rest and relax.

But if our foundational existence is 'fear' or 'insecurity', then when we motivate ourselves to achieve, conquer and be the best, we are also overworking the SNS. We are fighting a war within, basically. If you are constantly steeped in a nerve-wracking existence, your body and mind will eventually succumb to the stressors.

That's what happened to the young and talented Jennifer Capriati who, at 13, was the youngest to play professional tennis. She quickly climbed to the top 10 and, at the age of 16, she won a gold medal in the Olympics. But the rigours of professional tennis got to her eventually; drug overdoses and arrests for shoplifting brought her the wrong sort of attention. She admitted in an interview that she had even contemplated suicide due to tennis burnout. To her credit though, she slowly picked up her life and, in five years, returned to championship form. She went on to become world number one. She is a member of the International Tennis Hall of Fame.

RECEIVE GRACE WITH SELF-ACCEPTANCE

Our body has the natural ability to regulate its inner environment and ensure stability even amid fluctuations in the external situation. This natural rhythm is in sync with the Universe; when we eat, sleep and live a regulated life, we ensure a homoeostatic balance. Unfortunately, for many, an unrealistic ambition disturbs this balance. They invite stress-induced diseases and habits that could be totally avoided. Of course, that would mean fewer medals and perhaps no glory at all. But if 'achieving' is your mantra, you can't blame anyone else for your misery.

On the other hand, when you receive grace and lead a life of quiet acceptance, you align your body and mind with the larger plan. If my foundational existence is that of self-acceptance, I am content. In that state, I give my best; then even my profession becomes a spiritual experience. I am grateful in victory and gracious in defeat; there's no fear of the enemy because I am complete. I don't need the world to endorse my views, fans to applaud my success or television coverage to make me feel worthy.

The basic point is that if I accept myself, I will give my best and may even attract success. However, the reverse theory that is notoriously common is a dangerous notion to uphold. Most people imagine external success will help them achieve inner acceptance. Their self-worth is unfortunately dependent on a gold medal rather than on their own goodness.

In 1922, while staying at the Imperial Hotel in Tokyo, Albert Einstein realized he didn't have loose change to tip the bellboy who had delivered a message to him. Einstein instead tipped the boy with his theory of happiness that he scribbled on a piece of paper. The note was sold in 2018 for $1.5 million. This is what it said:

'A calm and modest life brings more happiness than the pursuit of success combined with constant restlessness.'

Jay shared another secret that afternoon in the Himalayas: 'Remember, my friend, we are alone in our life's journey. Just stay kind to yourself, and you'll do good to others as well.'

The next chapter shares simple techniques to cultivate humility.

SUMMARY

- The Himalayan life practice is:
  - Walk through life at a speed that is natural to you.
  - Don't compare yourself with others.
  - Don't stop.
- Real success is dependent on how you 'receive' life, not in how you 'achieve' it.
- When intensity becomes the norm, we disturb the natural ability of the body to regulate its inner environment.
- Instead of external success, we need to focus on inner self-acceptance, and that will lead to sustained success.

CHAPTER THIRTEEN

Humility Determines Your Success and Self-worth

'When King Prithu spoke, it's the humility in his speech that pleased the audience.'

– Srimad Bhagavatam (4.16.1)

IF YOU DO WHAT you commit to, you improve your self-worth and confidence.

Let's say you write down the following things in your journal: 'Today, I shall exercise, call three friends and appreciate them for their services, abstain from using my WhatsApp and Facebook for six hours.'

At 10 p.m., just before you retire for the day, you can revisit the journal and review the day's activities.

If a friend betrays his promise to you, your confidence in him is likely to fall. Likewise, if you break your promise to yourself, your belief in yourself will be negatively affected. Ironically, we often set ourselves high targets or unrealistic ambitions, and the result is that our sense of worth gradually wanes if we fail to achieve these ambitions.

THE BALANCE BETWEEN AMBITION
AND SMALLNESS

The solution is simple: Humbly accept one's insignificant position, and move forward with little but sure steps.

Often, when we have big dreams, we forget how small our position is. And, conversely, if we lack aspiration, we ignore our potential. The challenge is to balance ambition with being sensible. Just because you want to fly high doesn't mean you have wings; your feet need to be firmly grounded in reality.

A teenager I knew wanted to be the next Messi or Ronaldo. I asked him why he wanted to be a football star. He felt discouraged. I clarified that there's nothing wrong with his desire, but the whys and hows need to follow our ambition; otherwise, it remains a dream. And when you answer these painful questions, you face your inadequacies and see the agonizing distance between where you are now and where you want to be. And then you can start taking definite steps, even if they are small, on your journey forward.

There are many people who don't realize their talent because they feel they will never be able to succeed. For example, I have talked to budding sportsmen who feel that there is no point in pursuing their sport, because they feel they don't have the potential or because the competition is too much or some such thing. I reason with them that their talents have nothing to do with other sportspeople. They have to realize their own God-given gifts. And, to consummate their faculties, they merely need to move forward, slowly and surely.

HUMILITY IS THE FOUNDATION

An Indian folktale highlights the need to cultivate humility even amid success.

A kind-hearted, wealthy man once saw a young orphan and offered him help. He provided education to the boy, a job, a good income, a place to stay, food and love. The boy learnt fast and soon won the man's trust.

Years passed and the young man was given more significant responsibilities. Finally, he was given the coveted position of treasurer in the man's business. Other employees who had been working for many years felt envious and complained to the owner. The man patiently explained to them that this young man was like his son; not only was he competent, he also had an excellent character. The others weren't satisfied and alleged that the young man was quietly siphoning off the employer's funds. At night when everyone had left the premises, he would quietly sneak into a chamber, open a box and put his money there, they claimed. His hushed and mysterious movements confirmed that he was cheating his benevolent benefactor. Finally, urged by the staff, the man laid a trap and, just when the young man opened his secret chest, his detractors, led by the owner, caught him red-handed.

But what did they discover? To their shock, he had opened a case that contained the old, torn clothes that he was wearing when the man had found him on the street years ago. The boy explained to the bewildered group that he came here daily before closing the office to see his past so that he never forgot it. He didn't want to forget his humble roots and take the love and trust showered on him for granted.

His gratitude silenced his critics and earned him deep respect from his benefactor. Eventually, he inherited the entire fortune.

But naturally, we can't achieve humility as if it's a medal. The moment you think you are humble, you are likely to lose it. A town council once awarded a man for being the humblest person, but soon withdrew the award when the man wore the badge of humility on his shirt. He proclaimed to the world that he was the humblest man in the Universe and that, of all the good qualities he possessed, humility was his most cherished virtue!

A DAILY TEST TO CULTIVATE HUMILITY

My mentor in the monastery taught me a simple humility test to gauge my progress. He said I could ask myself three questions before I retired each night:

1. How much did I serve others today, and how much service did I receive from others?
2. Did I appreciate others today or seek appreciation for myself?
3. Was I concerned for others and remembered God, or was I been absorbed in myself?

The answer to these three questions helps me go deeper into my own motivations and mission in life. Many people secretly desire to be somebody important and contribute something significant. But to rise higher, we first need to descend into ourselves to examine our value systems.

You may plan to build a tower that will pierce the clouds, but first you need to lay the foundation of humility. And it's not easy – nothing good in this world is. But the good news is that when you walk the path of humility, the only competition you have is yourself.

You might wonder if humility will throttle your ambitions. The truth is that it will not. As the last chapter of this section will reveal, you can actually grow 'big' when you think small.

SUMMARY

- It's important to remain humble to sustain success.

CHAPTER FOURTEEN

Think Small, Grow Big

'The tiny fish in the cupped palms of King Satyavrata grew big to occupy a water pot, then a lake, a river and finally rose hundreds of miles long.'

– Srimad Bhagavatam (8.24)

ONE DAY, A CROW felt despondent. 'I am neither beautiful, nor can I sing well; I am just a dirty scavenger and people always shoo me away,' he said sadly to himself. Just then, seeing a beautiful swan, he sighed aloud, 'Oh! How attractive you are, with sparkling white feathers and an elegant gait. You live in a beautiful lake amid blooming lotuses and are admired by all.'

The swan humbly bowed his head and said, 'My dear friend, I am just a bland, unattractive, white-coloured bird. But just look at the parrot! He is beautifully green, and his reddish beak and sweet voice makes him an ideal choice for a pet; they are the most pampered among bird lovers.'

The crow soon met a parrot and showered praises on him for being the most blessed of birds. 'I feel incomplete,' confessed the parrot. 'I envy the multi-coloured feathers of a peacock. He is undoubtedly the most beautiful creature and when he spreads his feathers to dance during the rain, it's the most beautiful sight to behold.'

The crow rushed to meet the lucky peacock, and was surprised to find him miserable as well. 'I have no privacy; people keep looking for me, hunters poach my feathers and sell me to zoos,' he lamented. 'You are the luckiest; no one disturbs you. How I wish I was a carefree, happy crow flying everywhere just like you!'

Do you feel inadequate like the crow and believe that if you had something that someone else has you'd be happier? Do you grieve over the fact that people don't accept you for the way you are? The crow, the parrot, the swan and the peacock are all unique – and so are you. There is no need to hold back your originality and uniqueness. You are indeed special and you add to the sparkle of this world.

Remember, what water can do, gasoline can't; and what copper can do, gold cannot. The ant's tenderness helps it move about, while the tree's rigidity keeps it rooted. Each one of us has been designed to be utterly unique; there's a purpose that you alone can fulfil by being your distinctive self. You are here to be you... just you!

In the history of this Universe, there has been nobody like you, and in the infinity of time to come, there will not be another person like you. Yes, you are a wonder. So please celebrate, with gratitude, your unique contribution to this world.

HOW ACCEPTANCE HELPS

Acceptance means to know one's limitations, which are part of one's uniqueness, and be happy about them. For instance, I always wanted to write a lot and thought I could do it. It was only when I finally accepted that I am small and came to terms with my inability to write as much as I thought I should that I felt liberated. I set a simple, achievable target of 50 words daily, and as I began writing, I felt happy in doing just that much.

This is acceptance.

If I were to give up my writing totally, then that is not acceptance; if writing defines who I am, then by not writing I will simply lead a life of non-acceptance.

Interestingly, when we accept our insignificant place in this giant cosmos, we also become empowered to contribute much more than what we have so far. That's because we are happy in a state of acceptance. And happiness helps us give back to the Universe.

THE 'SMALL' VS. 'BIG' PARADIGM

A typical self-help guru or a life coach will prod you to 'think big'. For a change, try the recipe of 'thinking small' and see the difference.

'Big' refers to a lofty goal, an ideal that you wish you lived by. 'Small', however, is easy and you can achieve it even if you are sick or terribly busy.

Let's say you wish to lose 20 kg and be slim and fit. You make a grand plan that includes a daily workout of an hour. What happens? A few weeks later, you realize that in the midst of your erratic schedule, you haven't exercised at all. You again resolve to lose weight and make another plan, yet slip after a few days. If you have ever struggled to keep up with your plans, your life coach will suggest you practise strong determination or make your purpose stronger.

Most people, however, are unaware that willpower is a limited resource, and that the more we use determination during the day, the more the resource depletes and leaves us with 'decision fatigue' at the end of the day. If you have been frustrated in the past with plans failing repeatedly, try something new now.

Resolve right now that whatever happens, you'll exercise daily for just two minutes. Yes, you read that right – only two minutes. And you will do it even if the heavens fall! There's no meditation on your 'why', or purpose. You simply have no choice but to do it daily. But you choose a target that is so easy you just can't miss it. I first learnt of this technique when I saw a YouTube video by Stephen Guise, and it instantly resonated with me.

What happens when you think small is this: while doing

your two minutes of exercise, you'll likely feel nourished and comfortable to stretch a little more, and before you know it, you'll have done a full 10 minutes of exercise. But your minimum still remains two minutes. On some occasions, you may even go up to one hour but that's not because you had to do it; it's because you *wanted* to do it! There was no pressure, no intense willpower being summoned.

In fact, as you become comfortable with two minutes of exercise, you become curious to explore more. A sense of enjoyment and excitement pushes you to do more! The stretching of the body releases endorphins; you feel happy and are tempted to do more of the same activity. This tactic is safe and effective.

A PERSONAL TRANSFORMATION

I have a daily schedule of spiritual practice which begins at 4 a.m. For the last two decades, I have lived in a monastery where we chant, pray and meditate collectively. One important item on this list is to chant the holy names softly, using our beads, for over two hours. We repeat an ancient mantra over 1,500 times and keep a simple counting process that tells us when we have done our quota. We often hear in classes – and also individually affirm – that we need to be 'present' during our chanting, and that being 'here in the now' is the essence of this sacred practice.

Yet, 'attention' is easier said than done in this age of massive distractions. Even monks in a monastery can be victims of social media, WhatsApp and a plethora of other mindless activities that drain away the ability to be attentive. I become discouraged when my mind runs riot during the chanting, and the session becomes a mere ritual that needs to be done with. The heart isn't experiencing the sublime glories of the holy names that we hear from our scriptures.

One evening, I figured that the gap between the attention I wish I had daily and the harsh reality of being terribly distracted could be bridged by a simple method.

I decided to not worry about being attentive through all 1,500 mantras and just get five mantras done attentively. As I slowly and consciously invested my attention and prayer on the holy names, the five chants of those ancient sounds nourished me. I was tempted to chant another one. The extra one I chanted was because I wanted to and not because I had to or because I had vowed to.

Slowly, I realized that I was chanting more than 50 to 60 attentive mantras during my two-hour session. That's a 3 per cent attention rate, which is a big deal. Compared to the dry ritual that my spiritual practice had become, now I was chanting 3 per cent of my mantras attentively! Yet, I stuck to my minimum of five. Then even if the mind wandered, I wouldn't be harsh on myself; I'd accept my inattention.

I once read the story of a man who took his cat outside in the snow. As he placed her on the street, the cat stood stunned for a few seconds. Then she ran back inside the house. Later, he tried something different; he placed her at the door of the house. The cat slowly and curiously explored the doorstep. Then she gradually made her way down the steps. Eventually, she walked to the snow on the road and was soon wandering about happily in it. The cat's comfort zone had expanded because her owner had placed her near her comfort zone, and she was able to do as much as she was comfortable doing. This gave her the courage to explore more and more.

Similarly, if we place our schedules close to the mind's comfort, we'll see them as achievable; and slowly, we will begin to move outside our comfort zone. There is an inner assurance that if things get tough, you can rush back to a space you know you are comfortable in.

As I explored my capacity with the chanting, I was amazed to find that my zone kept expanding. Now I can happily chant more and more mantras attentively, for it isn't a drag any more.

ACCEPTANCE IS THE SOLUTION

I confess that, initially, it was a challenge for my mind and my ego to admit that I was 'small' and could not do much – for example, that I could only chant five mantras attentively. I'd often say in my lectures that one needs to chant their prayers attentively, yet now I was reducing the standard for myself. But it was more practical and achievable, and I understood that if one aimed too high at a time when one wasn't ready, a fall was quite likely!

As I've shared earlier, when my mind wandered during our two-hour chanting session, I'd gently reassure myself that it was all right as long as I had done five chants with love and attention. My acceptance of my real position, rather than hankering for what I should be, was a great relief.

Acceptance helped me aspire for more. I am sure if you went for one push-up a day, it would do the same to you. If you are struggling with poor determination, that could be because you always thought of yourself as a health freak. But remember this is your imagined identity, of what you would love to be, rather than what you are right now. You may not be as strong or as great as you wish you were, but by accepting your present situation, you are gently but truly moving forward.

REMEMBER AND CELEBRATE THE SMALL SUCCESSES

Good habits become difficult to cultivate because the mind has a strange proclivity to ruminate over past failures. Often, people claim that they want to be happy, but little do they realize that the mind relishes, with equal ferocity, even the pain of past suffering.

Therefore, if we really want to be happy, we need to remember the success and happy moments much more often. If we set small, achievable targets and achieve them with ease, the mind has a success to celebrate.

For example, you know now that my writing used to be erratic and inconsistent. On some days I wrote 5,000 words and then for months, I wrote nothing at all. As a result, I wrote little, although I wished I wrote more. My ambitions were inconsistent with my efforts.

My misery ended forever when one evening I resolved to do the following two things:

1. I accepted that I was not an accomplished writer. I was small and insignificant, yet I was happy the way God has made me, still complete and perfect.

2. I decided to write just 50 words daily. This was something I could do easily, and while I might write more on some days, that then was just a bonus. My target was no longer the 'great Indian novel' or 50,000 words every month. I realized my earlier goals were not only unrealistic but also stress-inducing.

What happened?

I wrote a lot more than 50 words. But I kept reminding myself that I was exceeding my target and that I didn't need to. I was happy to write more because I was good at it and was doing better than my target.

My mind has less reason to rant and fret now. Sometimes it prods me to raise my target and write more, but I know that my mind is just cheating me.

In the past, I had higher targets but wrote little. Now, with little targets, I am writing so much more. Hence, I figured that it's better to under-promise and over-deliver when it comes to dealing with the mind.

My most precious realization in life is that when I am happy with my success, I can contribute and achieve so much more.

Now that you have learnt tools to practise awareness and acceptance, you are ready to shoot for the stars – it's your vision to succeed that ultimately helps you live beyond your mind.

And that's the subject of Section 3: Aspiration.

SUMMARY

- Instead of thinking big and having lofty targets, let's try thinking small for a change.
- When we set achievable targets, we accept our small position and also feel happy. It's easier to achieve our targets when they are realistic and manageable.
- Determination is a limited resource, and the more we exhaust it, the more likely we are to be affected by decision fatigue.
- Slowly venturing out of our comfort zone is a better strategy than going too far out, only to revert to previous habits.

SECTION 3

Aspiration

'I shall cross over the insurmountable ocean of nescience with my firm determination...'

— Srimad Bhagavatam (11.23.57)

CHAPTER ONE

Marry a Purpose

'Those who are on this path are resolute in purpose, and their aim is one. O beloved child of the Kurus, the intelligence of those who are irresolute is many-branched.'
— Bhagavad Gita (2.41)

ONCE THE GATES OF Raigad Fort were closed at sunset, no one could enter or leave the fort. These were Shivaji's orders. Hirkani, a milk vendor from the nearby village of Pachad, found herself stuck inside one evening. Like others who came into the fort daily to sell their wares, she had been busy selling milk, and realized a little too late that the gates had been locked for the day. She pleaded with the guard to make an exception for her as her child would be hungry and waiting for her at home.

'Sorry, these are the orders of the Emperor himself,' declared the guard. 'They will now open only tomorrow morning.'

At almost 3,000 feet above sea level, the fort was located in the expansive Sahyadri mountains. It was said that no enemy could penetrate the fortress, but this was 1675, when the Mughals posed a real threat to Shivaji's reign. The guards couldn't take a chance; Hirkani would have to spend the night inside the fort. She, however, was determined to return home to her child.

Trying not to attract attention, Hirkani explored the fort and found that there were strong walls with 70-feet-high doors guarding the citadel on all sides. There was clearly no escape possible through those doors. Eventually, she discovered that on one side there was actually no wall because the steep mountainside made it impossible for anyone to scale it.

Hirkani peered over the edge; the sheer drop was terrifying. She broke into a sweat. If soldiers couldn't take on that climb, how could she even contemplate it? But then she thought of her little one, and she knew her longing to get home was stronger than her fear. Her mind cleared; she knew what she had to do, and she was determined to succeed.

Hirkani began to descend in the dark, placing each foot carefully on that treacherous mountain, warding off the bats that flew around her. After what seemed like an eternity, her feet touched the ground, and she ran home.

The next morning, this brave woman was back at the fort to sell milk. The guard recognized her immediately and raised an alarm. Hirkani was produced before Shivaji, who was outraged. 'Even the mightiest can't break my security systems; so how could you, a simple woman, do so?' He then asked her to take him to the spot from where she had made her escape the previous night.

Hirkani took Shivaji to the wall. He took in the imposing sight below; and was absolutely astonished. Then he asked her if she could repeat the feat for him. She moved to the edge confidently but, upon looking down, froze in horror. 'No, my king,' she cried out, 'I can't do it now.' Shivaji smiled as understanding dawned upon him. He knew, seeing her scratched hands and torn clothes, that she was speaking the truth about the previous night. Her desire to return to her child had been so strong that she had been able to transcend her fear.

Shivaji renamed the spot 'Hirkani Burj' (Hirkani's bastion) in her honour.

A PASSION TO LIVE FOR

A person obsessed with a cause is likely to ignore the mind's fears and insecurities. Hirkani desperately wanted to be with her child and, therefore, her mind refused to see the task as impossible. It's amazing how the mind cooperates when you rise to pursue a goal beyond the mind, beyond the self even. Hirkani's single-minded determination to a cause higher than herself lifted her beyond the mind's conditioning.

A clarification is in order here: A sudden high dopamine and adrenaline rush can also propel you to transcend your fear in a certain moment, but this is just a passing phenomenon and can't be sustained. To *live* a whole life beyond the mind requires you to marry a purpose, one that you are willing to die for.

If you are desperate to travel to a certain place knowing a treasure awaits you there, will you complain about the food served on the flight? No. You're excited about reaching your destination, and that's all that really matters. Likewise, life is a glorious adventure with unlimited opportunities for growth and fulfilment. And, for those desperate to grab the jewels of realization, the daily trifles don't matter.

Hirkani's love for her child compelled her to perform an incredible task. On the other hand, there are many people endowed with talents and abilities, yet they allow their minds to be overwhelmed by worries and doubts. As a result, they miss the opportunities waiting for them.

In fact, the most successful men and women in the world are ordinary souls but with extraordinary passions and aspirations. Albert Einstein, regarded as one of the greatest physicists who ever walked on earth, was an average man. He loved music, lacked sophistication or worldliness, and had a child-like simplicity. Today, however, Einstein is regarded as a genius. His friend Robert Oppenheimer revealed the secret: Einstein was profoundly stubborn. Einstein himself confessed, 'I have no special talents. I am only passionately curious.'

๛

Have you noticed how even a terribly destructive purpose can help one move beyond the mind? An innocent teenager, recruited by the agents of hate, allows his tender heart to get corrupted. He then becomes a vicious terrorist, killing innocents and performing dastardly acts, which he would have never done had he not been 'brainwashed'. In committing these heinous crimes, it may appear that he has transcended the fear of losing his own life.

In contrast to a radicalized terrorist, Mahatma Gandhi was a timid and unsuccessful lawyer. His poor oratory didn't help him either. However, he eventually devoted his life to a single pursuit: the independence of his motherland from British rule. The rest is history. Gandhiji's cause and mission inflamed the hearts of 300 million Indians with a desire for Swaraj, self-rule and complete independence from the British Empire.

FROM MINDLESS WORRY TO PURPOSEFUL ACTION

If you hold a 10-rupee coin close to your eyes, your vision of the sun is blocked. There's no comparison of their sizes – the gigantic ball of fire is a quadrillion times bigger than a tiny piece of steel. Still, a four-gram coin, when close to your eyes, can block your vision of the colossal sun. Often, you are so preoccupied with your daily worries that it blocks your vision of the big picture that is life. Yet, your larger vision of life is a far more significant reality than a harsh comment by a colleague or the haughty man who drove past you shrieking expletives.

You may claim it is impossible not to worry. Yes, worry is like a bird that flies over your roof – you can't really prevent that, but you can definitely stop her from building a nest there. And the strength to thwart the mind's attempt to build a nest comes when you have a raging fire of purpose inside you.

If you lack drive, you will drift away whenever the waves of desire pull at you. Riding the mind's chariot, those with a paucity of passion remain ever dissatisfied. For them, life is simply a series of unfortunate events that 'happens' to them. On the other hand, when you lead a life of purpose, you *make* things happen.

When you have a dream and a willingness to live for it, the mind doesn't matter. The Bhagavad Gita (2.41) offers sagacious words: 'Those who are on this path are resolute in purpose, and their aim is one...the intelligence of those who are irresolute is many-branched.'

There are some people who have a vision but also live with the illusion that they are making a sacrifice and doing something wonderful. The next chapter challenges such a faulty mindset.

SUMMARY

- When you are deeply connected to a purpose, the mind doesn't worry about how difficult a task is. Further, petty issues become irrelevant. Brilliant and successful people like Albert Einstein and Mahatma Gandhi didn't care about their ordinariness and lack of skills; they simply let the flames of their passion burn strong.
- Worry is like holding a 10-rupee coin close to your eyes – it blocks the larger perspective of life.

CHAPTER TWO

The Falsehood of Sacrifice and the Need for Self-care

'He who is regulated in his habits of eating, sleeping, recreation and work can mitigate all material pains by practicing the yoga system.'

– Bhagavad Gita (6.17)

ANUP SINHA, A FRIEND of mine in his early forties, asked in a voice choked with emotion, 'I always serve others selflessly; yet, I am unhappy. Why is this so?'

'What do you mean you are selfless? What do you do?' I asked quietly.

Anup told me about his life: He had been responsible for getting eight siblings educated and married. All this had kept him so busy that he had never married. Besides, he was upset that his family was ungrateful for all he had done for them. In fact, they still wanted money, and he was always arranging it for them. He claimed he had sacrificed his health, wealth and time for his family, but they only want more and more. He said, 'My health is a mess now; my blood pressure and sugar levels are abnormally high. I also feel lonely and have no free time to read or have fun.'

I blurted out in surprise, 'Why did you do all this?'

'To serve my family and make them happy.'

I persisted with my line of reasoning. 'But *why* did you do it?'

'Because that's the right thing to do, isn't it? We should be selfless and care for our near and dear ones.'

'Are you saying it's wrong to care for oneself and one's own need for good health, companionship, freedom and happiness?' I asked.

He was embarrassed. 'Well, yeah, I guess I should have taken care of myself too.'

'Then why didn't you?' Now I was sure I was annoying him with my questions.

He pondered for a few seconds. 'Hmm, let me see. I thought I was selfish if I did anything that made me happy.'

'Did you ever realize there's a difference between being selfish and taking care of yourself – self-care?'

'No!' He looked astonished. And then, as this revelation began to sink in, I saw his face break open into a wide smile.

SELF-CARE VS. BEING SELFISH

If you ignore your finances, health or well-being because you believe that this is the way to be selfless, you are actually being foolish. If you don't take care of yourself, who will? And unless you take care of yourself, how can you look after anyone else? This is a simple example, but you'll get my point: On a flight, you're told to put on your oxygen mask before you attend to your child.

If the busy 'Anups' of the world are going to ignore themselves while looking after others, they better learn not to complain. But they must realize that all they are worth then is a candle that melts away even as it brings light to the room. Is this sacrifice worth it? If you still persist in giving to others without giving to yourself, be aware of the price you are paying for your decision, and be happy about it.

According to me, to actively protect one's well-being and happiness, especially during periods of stress, is a sign of maturity, not selfishness. It's when we are inconsiderate to others' needs and can't think beyond 'I' and 'mine' that we are selfish. Otherwise, to care for your own self is not only natural but also an absolute necessity. Anup believed his happiness lay in his family's well-being, but the fact that he was miserable proves his theory wrong. The converse theory holds true for the likes of Anup: Your family's happiness lies in *your* well-being! Anup needs to be kinder to himself. If his care doesn't include himself, his service is *incomplete*!

THE FALSEHOOD OF SACRIFICE

I was once honoured in front of a large gathering of about five thousand people for my 'selfless service'. (I was visiting their village to give them a series of lectures.) As the audience clapped and cheered, and the host praised me, I enjoyed every moment of the attention. A few seconds later, I was given the mic to say a few concluding words. I spoke automatically, as though following a ritual rather than speaking with heartfelt emotion. I talked about how my greatest happiness lay in serving them, and urged them to let me visit the town year after year, for I sought nothing but the opportunity to give back. The crowd now roared in approval; my lecture had pleased them, and now my 'humility' and 'sacrifice' had won them over.

After the event, hundreds swarmed towards the stage and thanked me. I returned to my room exhausted. As I lay down to rest, I heard a soft voice within congratulating me: Oh that was a great political speech today! I ignored the voice and closed my eyes. But sleep eluded me, and I just tossed and turned. Slowly, an anxious thought gripped me. Had I come to the village because I really wanted to 'sacrifice' and 'serve', or was there more to it?

I examined myself to find the real reason for my visit. The truth is that I had come to this remote place because of its scenic beauty, the river, and the clean air. I had come here for the solitude that nourished me and helped give back meaningfully to the villagers. Thus the essential motivation was not sacrifice but my own needs. Instead, I had presented my visit as if I was a tireless missionary who lived for others, even at a personal inconvenience.

I accepted this realization about myself without any judgement. This was a choice I had, a choice we all have in *every* moment – to accept ourselves just as we are, or to judge and criticize ourselves. Judgement will not let us move forward and grow. It is accepting the self, no matter what mistake has been made, that lets us move on and change, if we choose to. Although I had lied to myself, I now felt relieved at my acceptance of the truth. I was no messiah; I was an ordinary man whose needs had been fulfilled in the scenic countryside and, as a mark of gratitude, I had served them for their kindness. Connecting to this fact filled me with peace, and a heavy weight was lifted from my shoulders.

I slept deeply after that. The next morning, I resolved I would not give a politician's speech extolling 'sacrifice' ever again.

OFFER WHAT YOU HAVE, NOT WHAT YOU DON'T

You don't need to give up what you love and what you are good at for an imaginary noble cause. It's better to excel at your core talent and offer *that* as a service, than promise something you don't actually possess.

Mother Teresa used to tell people to do even little things with great love. Let's be honest and do what we love, and somewhere on our journey we can offer that talent to bring goodness into this world. In the Bhagavad Gita, Lord Krishna chastised Arjuna because he was attempting to be what he was not. Arjuna had decided to leave the battlefield and become a mendicant. Krishna warned him that he was a warrior by nature, and if he renounced the war and went into the forest, he would bring about massive ruin in the social fabric.

LIVING FOR THE SELF!

While it is healthy to accept with gratitude the sacrifice and kindness that others may give us, it's dangerous to think *we* are doing the same for others. If I imagine I am living for others, I tend to invite false pride. I may also overlook the kindness others are showering upon me abundantly. Instead, if I am honest about taking care of my needs, I'll likely be humble and grateful to those who help me.

Three decades ago, a famous Indian cricket player was accused of match-fixing and bribery. As an impressionable teenager, the incident affected me profoundly, especially when the man broke down, denying the allegations. He declared, 'I lived, breathed and played for my country, and have carried the burden of the nation for so many years. I shall take sannyasa – accept renunciation by leaving family and society – if the charges are not withdrawn.'

I remember my dad's cynical observation then: 'He played not for the nation but himself. Every player serves his own needs, and if it happens to please the country, that is welcome. But the essential motivation is his passion for the sport and not his service to the country.'

He then said to no one in particular, 'Accept it and be gracious. You do things because you *want* to, not because you want to sacrifice.'

Today, in my own life, this rings true. I do things because I want to and I am glad I can serve others as well. A valuable lesson I learned during my trip to the village was that it is more honourable to live for oneself with gratitude than to live for the false ego, with the illusion of service and sacrifice.

But are there people who sacrifice their lives for their country or family? Is it for real? Yes, it is, and it is one of the two types of happiness that we will explore in the next chapter.

SUMMARY

- To care for others, you need to first care for yourself.
- Self-care turns to selfishness if we can't think beyond 'I' and are inconsiderate to the needs and concerns of others.
- Connecting to the truth of our needs rather than the lie of sacrifice relieves us of the emotional burden of living a lie.

CHAPTER THREE

Two Levels of Happiness

'Happiness and sadness come and go like the summer and winter; they arise out of sense perception, O Arjuna, just tolerate them!'

— Bhagavad Gita (2.14)

SANJAY KUMAR WAS A taxi driver who struggled to make ends meet. He dreamed of joining the Indian army, but had failed to do so despite three attempts. On his fourth attemmpt, he finally made it to the 13th Battalion J & K Rifles.

During the Kargil War in July 1999, Sanjay was in charge of a team of men, and their mission was to wrest an area from Pakistani soldiers at Mushkoh valley. He single-handedly charged at the enemy, with utter indifference to his own safety, and took bullets in his chest and forearm. Despite his injuries, he continued to fight, killing three enemy soldiers and attacking a bunker. His courage frightened the enemy, and as they fled his men charged and captured the area. For his exceptional courage, this brave soldier was awarded the Param Vir Chakra.

Sanjay chose a career that could threaten his very life, but he loved what he did. Serving in the army was the vision he lived for, and he gave it all he had. Today, he is a role model for many people.

When trapped in the daily routine, we tend to think like this:

'My life is already troubled; do not ask me about my goals and aspirations! I just want to be happy.'

Vedic literature offers an exciting paradigm shift. It tells us to forget happiness and seek a noble aspiration instead. A contribution to the world or leaving some sort of legacy behind is what will make you happy.

Happiness can be defined in two ways: One is pleasure, which you get when you gratify your senses; and the other is a profound sense of fulfilment you get when you pursue a worthy goal. A peg of whiskey or a delicious chocolate could tickle your senses, but that's fleeting. However, like Sanjay Kumar, if you choose to live beyond the little needs of the mind and body, you connect to a higher level of happiness. This kind of happiness can contribute to another's well-being and happiness as well.

At one level, happiness means pleasure. When you listen to a good song, eat a pizza, enjoy sex, receive love and appreciation, do what you like, or rest after a long day, your senses are pleased and you feel good. And everyone wants this because we are pleasure-seeking individuals by nature.

The search for happiness, when defined as pleasure, is common to all animals and humans. However, you'll notice that for almost all humans, this experience is brief. You won't feel happy each time you meet your loved one or eat a delicacy. In fact, your pleasure levels will fluctuate. And if your focus is happiness alone, as defined above, then you invite misery when you don't get it.

If the word happiness only means 'pleasure' to you, then you will only think of ways to stimulate the senses. And these stimulants are not as abundantly available as we'd like to imagine. Then, in a desperate attempt to be happy, you will start figuring out newer ways to squeeze out pleasure. As a result, you're likely to get sucked into a mire of stress. The more you struggle, the more you try to control your life, and the more agony you experience as a result. You thus land up far away from where you wanted to be initially.

That's when you realize happiness is a fleeting, elusive thing.

It's like the proverbial carrot dangling in front of the donkey, always out of reach, yet enticing enough to goad you on.

An Indian folktale reveals the nature of pleasure in this world. During a long journey through the forest, a tired man begged God to grant him a horse so he didn't have to walk. Soon, a mare appeared, and he rode happily on her back. However, his happiness was short-lived as the mare was pregnant. When she gave birth to a foal, the man had to care for the foal as well as the mare, and this slowed him down and tired him out. Meanwhile, the horse reluctantly carried the man along the forest path.

Every pleasure that we experience is pregnant like this horse, carrying with it a consequence for the future. In fact, life is like that; there are struggles at every stage. What makes life beautiful though is aspiration.

The overall effect of this search for happiness is that it takes a heavy toll on the SNS. Since there is not much time to relax and slow down, the PSNS is imbalanced. As a result, burn out, breakdown and depression are common occurrences. Happiness then becomes a frantic pursuit for pleasure, and the body wears out faster and faster.

As opposed to momentary pleasures, there is another type of happiness based on values and purpose. It may seem abstract on the surface, but if we spend some quiet, solitary moments with ourselves, we will come to understand what defines us as individuals. The moment you remember your purpose – and you could write it down as a phrase, a poem or a sentence – it defines your being or who you essentially are, and you are then connected to your purpose.

But how is purpose related to happiness?

If you are conditioned to believe that happiness is merely of the superficial kind, then you'll be disappointed because there is no lasting happiness in this world. But there *is* deep contentment when you live your mission. Just as suffering is evident and all-pervasive, contentment can also be perceived by the way people lead their lives.

Usha Mataji was 96 years old when I met her for the first time. I interviewed her for our local community magazine as she was one of the most enthusiastic participants in our spiritual gatherings. She hadn't missed a single pilgrimage in decades. When she was focused on prayer, her beads in her hands, she spoke little. In her presence, I felt the same peace that I'd feel sitting under the giant 300-year-old banyan tree close to our monastery. She seemed timeless too.

I asked her once if her life had seen its ups and downs. She laughed and said, 'Only downs!' Then she said quietly, 'What could be more painful for a mother than to see four of her children die before her?' I was stunned at the kind of pain she must have endured. Yet, she had chosen to live a full life of service and love. In her offering and grateful contribution to others, there was only grace and dignity. Perhaps she experienced no pleasure for days together; and yet, she felt her life was full of joy.

To live a happy life, we need a sense of purpose and a calm acceptance of the hardships that will definitely come to us.

If a purpose-driven life guarantees a deeper level of happiness, how do you discover *your* purpose? The next chapter shares tools for you to discover your vision through the practice of Bhakti yoga.

SUMMARY

- The two levels of happiness are pleasure and a life of purpose. The former is experienced when we tickle our senses through food, films, sex and so on. This experience is not only fleeting but also wanes with time. A life of purpose is what brings real meaning and contentment.

CHAPTER FOUR

Bhakti Yoga to Find Your Purpose

'Learn the truth from the learned, but with humble inquiry and service.'

– Bhagavad Gita (4.34)

I KNEW A YOUNG man who felt he was unable to understand the meaning and purpose of his life, and he was very unhappy as a result. I asked him if he was keen to know the meaning of his life, and he said an emphatic yes. 'Congratulations!' I said. 'That's your purpose.'

What makes us different from animals is our ability to seek a purpose beyond eating, sleeping, sex and defending our territory; we can use our intelligence and skills to make a positive difference in the world.

The challenge for many people is simply to discover this purpose. With the surfeit of distractions around us, it's natural to find people confused about what they really want to do in life.

The path of Bhakti yoga has two principal methods that will help you discover your purpose. The first is chanting God's holy names and listening to the sacred scriptures. The second is doing service for others.

Adolf Hitler was an introspective person; he also wrote extensive diaries. Over two turbulent decades of history (1925–45), he wrote almost 10 books. However, during the same period, he initiated the Second World War and murdered over 5 million Jews. Another 20 million civilians and prisoners of war were killed by the Nazis. The moral of the story is that without an evolved *conscience*, mere introspection is dangerous.

The practices of journal writing and introspection are incomplete without humbly entering a sacred wisdom space. You can do this by absorbing the words of the scriptures, holy books and revered saints. As Stephen Covey points out in his all-time classic, *The Seven Habits of Highly Effective People*, Hitler had self-awareness, imagination and will power, but absolutely no conscience. It's this critical factor that aligns your consciousness to the 'true north' or universal principles, so that your purpose adds meaning and joy to the lives of others along with yourself.

If you live trapped in the mind's likes and dislikes – the duality of this world – you cannot access the soul's wisdom. We enter a spiritual space when we 'receive' direction from a realm beyond the reach of the mind–intelligence–ego. These are life-enhancing universal principles that we need to access. That is why many religious traditions focus on obtaining this grace.

BHAKTI YOGA PRACTICES

The practice of Bhakti yoga teaches us to connect with God and humanity through the language of love. The varied methods on this path help one discover one's true self and unique purpose in life.

An essential practice among Bhakti spiritualists is 'hearing' or submissive aural reception to spiritual wisdom. This could either be done by studying sacred books like the Bhagavad Gita, or hearing other practitioners speak from these books. This is a daily ritual in most temples and ashrams, and the class is usually well attended by the members of the monastery as well as the congregation.

Scriptural knowledge purifies the mind and intelligence in much the same way as fresh rain washes away the dirt accumulated on the leaves of a tree. Our consciousness is often contaminated with small biases and strong prejudices. We are like the proverbial 'frog in the well'; we imagine we are right while others are wrong. However, when we receive humbly, we express humility to the Universe. Our willingness to receive wisdom develops our 'wisdom body' and a strong intuition becomes a natural by-product of an attentive spiritual practice.

Chanting for Self-discovery

As described in the first section of this book, many spiritual traditions emphasize the chanting of mantras or divine incantations.

In the Bhakti yoga tradition I come from, we chant the 'Hare Krishna' mantra softly on our prayer beads. These prayers help us access the divine aspect of the self, which is known as the 'wisdom body'. From this realm of awareness, our life in this world is a sacred act of service. Members of our monastery begin their day with two hours of chanting the following mantra:

> *Hare Krishna Hare Krishna Krishna Krishna Hare Hare*
> *Hare Rama Hare Rama Rama Rama Hare Hare*

As we connect to the sound of this prayer, as we listen and receive the mantra, we also access the deeper meaning of this affirmation: *I want to serve and contribute*. This connects us to our internal compass; without a developed conscience, our introspection is like a ship without the guidance of a lighthouse.

Since the purpose is to serve, the details of how best one can do it are revealed in the course of time, but only if we add the all-important element of practical service.

Serve to Please

Many mistakenly believe that the knowledge of one's vision and purpose must precede effective action. Interestingly, the reverse works just as effectively: You can participate in a series of small acts of service, and then discover what you truly love or what your purpose is. Small acts of service, over time, give birth to love in the heart.

Glenn Teton was the only son of a respected Chicago lawyer. He met Bhaktivedanta Swami Srila Prabhupada in March 1969 while studying in Boston. Inspired by his teachings, Glenn joined the fledgling society and took the vows of dedicated service. He soon moved to Mumbai to help develop their community on a 4-acre plot. The work was difficult and the area lay in a remote part of the city. Besides unfriendly neighbours who suspected that foreigners like Glenn were CIA agents, the group had to also tackle issues such as shortage of water, lack of proper sewage, malaria and other tropical diseases, as well as attacks by the land mafia. However, Glenn and his team persevered, and today the ISKCON temple is one of the many landmarks in Mumbai. Glenn went on to become an initiated celibate monk and was later awarded 'sannyasa', the highest position in a renounced order. Since then he is respectfully called Giriraj Swami.

I once asked Giriraj Swami what was the love and purpose that burnt like a blazing fire within him. What inspired him to serve selflessly for over five decades? He said that what motivated him to serve was the opposite – consistent service over a long period of time. And this filled his heart with love!

A POTENT COMBINATION

How does the combination of studying the scriptures and service work?

Madan Mohan Malaviya, popularly known as Panditji, was a towering educationist and a leader in the Indian freedom struggle. He commanded the respect of stalwarts like Mahatma Gandhi and Rabindranath Tagore. He was also awarded the Bharat Ratna, India's highest civilian honour.

As a young boy, he learned Sanskrit and began to study the sacred Srimad Bhagavatam from his father, who spoke to him at length about the sacred scriptures. Later, he studied law, became the editor of popular newspapers, and founded the Banaras Hindu University – the largest residential university in Asia – which he headed for over two decades. Despite his sterling leadership qualities, he retired from his law practice at the high point of his career because he wanted to lead a life of silent social service and prayerful contemplation.

India, however, was not silent at that time; the country burned with violent protests, and the demand for freedom from the British Empire had reached its pitch.

Fourteen years passed and, in 1924, Madan Mohan Malaviya was remembered once again by the nationalist leaders. Over 170 men had been sentenced to the gallows by the British for burning a police post at Chauri-Chaura in Gorakhpur, and the Indian National Congress requested him to defend the case on their behalf.

Despite a hiatus from the law for over a decade, Panditji came back in style. So impressive were his presentations that the then Chief Justice, Sir Grimwood Mears, bowed thrice as a mark of great appreciation to the utter genius of his defence. More than 160 men were acquitted, and for the rest who were proven guilty and had been awarded the death sentence. Malviya managed to reduce their sentence to life imprisonment; all their lives were spared.

But even as a national hero, he remained firmly grounded. His inner state of spiritual purity and service was the secret to his success. He maintained his spiritual strength through an attitude of service, and his submissive reception to the scriptures.

One day, at the peak of his popularity, he had decided to learn the meaning of a few problematic verses of the Bhagavad Gita from a prolific Vedic scholar and celibate monk, Srila Bhaktisiddhanta Saraswati Thakur.

Bhaktisiddhanta, who lived in a simple ashram with his disciples, was unimpressed by Malaviya's academic and political achievements, and he confessed he was busy and wouldn't be able to answer his queries. He even suggested that he could meet his disciples in the monastery instead and learn from them.

Malaviya humbly approached the ashram monks, who were not only much younger and inexperienced in worldly ways, but also lacked Panditji's erudition. The monks said they were also busy and asked him if he would first help them clean the pots and the ashram premises; later, they could discuss the verses. Again, the great but humble scholar joined the monks in their chores, and several hours passed in joint services.

Five hours later, when they took a break, the monks asked Malaviya about his doubts. He gratefully confessed that during his service at the ashram, he had felt a cleansing of his heart; his misgivings had dissolved; and certain spiritual truths now shone within him as bright as the afternoon sun.

Thus, when humble chanting and listening to scriptures unites with real service, the result is ecstasy and selfless service.

But do the ancient scriptures contain solutions to modern-day problems? And, if they do, how do we discover them? Chapter 5 will answer this question.

SUMMARY

- Bhakti yoga endorses two practices that help us discover our purpose in life: Hearing and chanting of the holy names and the scriptures; and service towards others.

CHAPTER FIVE

Are Age-old Scriptures Practical in the Twenty-first Century?

'I live in everyone's heart and bring remembrance, knowledge and forgetfulness.'

— Bhagavad Gita (15.15)

'OH, THE CLASS WAS so practical,' complimented a friend after I offered eight tips to deal with the mind. 'The acronyms made it easier to remember.' A few others also thanked me, saying, 'The jokes were so funny!'

Seventy-five of us were on a pilgrimage to Sri Lanka, visiting the places mentioned in the Ramayana. I had given a discourse one day, and felt happy that it had been of some value.

However, the next morning, I was in for a surprise.

I narrated a section from the war episode between Rama and Ravana's armies, and saw my previously appreciative friends a little distracted. Some of them even struggled to stay awake in the class. I felt sorry for them, for I knew they must have heard the Ramayana a thousand times before.

As I hurried to my room after the talk, feeling a little discouraged, a different group of people came up to me and thanked me for a 'nourishing' sermon on the sacred compositions. 'It was beautiful,' one of them said. 'The Lord's pastimes bathed our consciousness with spiritual nectar.'

'But I have already given these lectures so many times,' I said, 'and you've heard the Ramayana since your childhood.'

'Yeah,' they beamed. 'All the same, it was so nice to hear it again.'

That evening, I realized that I had catered to two different needs during my lectures: one was the need for realistic, practical skills that had many takers; and the other was the hunger for spiritual nutrition, which is abstract and often intangible.

DO ANCIENT TEACHINGS MATTER IN MODERN TIMES?

When we hear or study the ancient stories of God and His devotees, we may well wonder how all this is relevant in our modern lives. Can we possibly apply these teachings to our day-to-day challenges?

Yes, we can and we must. Ancient wisdom is timeless, and we can find solutions to all our modern issues in books like the Bhagavad Gita. Many intelligent spiritual teachers, therefore, seek to connect ancient literature to our modern times; they help students move from the known to the unknown – from where they are to where the teacher wants them to go. My mentors in the monastery would rack their brains to make classical books exciting. They took us from things that were familiar and near to us to an unfamiliar territory far from our comprehension, and we travelled happily from what 'is' to what shall be! Hence, an effective leader knows that there is more to life than merely providing efficient solutions.

There is a flip side to this though for the pupil who waits to be spoon-fed by the instructor. He remains disconnected from his intuition and inner compass. The soul stays buried in the surfeit of pragmatic tips or the 'how to' points that the life coach provides. The disciple doesn't comprehend there is a guide *within* him who can help him discover answers to the perplexing problems of life.

Most pragmatic things that people share are inherently 'theirs', and may not necessarily help others. If you advocate the benefits of jogging daily, it may help a few people, but it will be of no use to a lame man. Each of us is made of a unique emotional and mental mix. Therefore, it is crucial that we connect to ourselves, to our own needs and problems, and to the required remedies in a particular time, place and circumstance.

For our inner world, a similar law works. Scriptures provide principles that you can distinctively apply, within reason and awareness, in your situation.

Sacred texts like the Ramayana, Mahabharata and the Bhagavad Gita help us access an *internal* guru. To understand what this inner preceptor is ready to teach us, we study or listen to old texts with attention and reverence. We open our hearts to access wisdom from an altogether different plateau.

Unfortunately, most of us live in our skulls, so much so that we only want skills! We can't think of a life beyond our struggles and needs. We continuously seek helpful tips to make our lives meaningful and better.

Wellness seminars and TED Talks meet this basic requirement. YouTube videos can teach you nearly everything – from how to learn to read and write, to making love, and even how to overcome a YouTube addiction! Ironically though, modern humans are as unhappy as the previous generation, if not unhappier. With no shortage of information available online on any subject matter, isn't it surprising that people are still unhappy?

No, not really. All things can't be known intellectually. We need to access and experience phenomena from a space beyond the cerebral region in order to evolve as human beings and find lasting contentment and peace in life.

Eknath was a great saint from Maharashtra. He arranged for his daughter to marry a pious man, who unfortunately fell into bad company. Every night, the young husband left home and returned in the wee hours of the morning. His concerned wife approached her father for help. Eknath called his son-in-law and asked him for a favour. 'My daughter is a fool, and you are a learned man. Please read just two verses of the Bhagavad Gita every night before you leave for your rendezvous.'

The young man obliged the sage. As he read daily, the words gradually transformed his heart, his conscience awakened, and his clarity and determination grew stronger. One night, he let go of his late-night adventures for good, and stayed home with his loving wife.

It's essential to go beyond mere information to a world of spiritual transformation. Besides, quick fixes won't have a profound effect on an individual as compared to their own 'aha' moments and precious personal discoveries. And the Srimad Bhagavatam and Bhagavad Gita assure you many epiphanies.

WINNING THE WAR OF LIFE

In every military academy, legendary battles are taught and studied extensively. Yet, each warrior knows that all combat is unique and that when he faces an enemy he can't browse through his notes to pick a method. Humbly studying past wars helps a military general sharpen his judgement and develop perception. He then decides a course of action based on the state of affairs where he trusts his gut and accumulated discernment over the years. The combination of experience, knowledge and careful assessment helps one make a decision on the spur of the moment.

We also struggle on the battlefield of our inner world, where one angry phone call from a friend can throw us into deep despair. A culture of scriptural study improves awareness and our ability to see situations and people through a larger perspective, beyond the seemingly obvious. We learn to look at a higher dimension of reality and redefine what is sacred and what is inconsequential in our lives. Based on this inner growth, we can decide our priorities and actions.

Unfortunately, we live in an age where speed, action and noise determine success. Insight, talent and happiness are all quantified on a scale of 1 to 10. From movies to your experience in a mall, or even your love life, everything is measured in numbers. When specifics rule the roost, there's no place for abstract principles. But many things in life – especially your tsunami of feelings and moods – are vague, and can't be computed objectively. To connect to your 'voice' in all the 'noise' outside is a real challenge, but vital in these times we're living in.

DEVELOPING THE WISDOM BODY

Let's look at cell differentiation. How is it that immediately after conception, cells know how to begin to grow and multiply? How is it that exactly the right number of cells forms the muscles, heart or brain? Where is this information coming from? Who is supplying it?

Thousands of such startling facts in nature point to a divine intelligence at play. Some call it God; others refer to it as Awareness or Universal Energy. Indian saints called it the 'Paramatma', 'super soul'. Whatever you call it, this force directs you the same way it directs a calf to find its mother amongst thousands of cows in a field.

The more pertinent question is whether we should trust this cosmic force. Do we trust ourselves? Can we align ourselves and our conscience and intuition to this force or Paramatma? The intensity of our daily lives creates an endless babble in our minds, blocking us from our own connection to our wisdom body. But there is one way in which we can retrieve our inner wisdom, and the key to this is to 'listen' or 'receive' wisdom from spiritual books.

Scriptures that speak of events that happened thousands of years ago are as relevant today as when they were first heard. The secret, however, is to read or hear them unhurriedly and attentively. Then, if something resonates, pause and allow yourself to recognize it. Allow the value or principle in a particular text to enter deeper into your heart. Gradually, but assuredly, you'll connect the passage to your situation. That is how scriptures help us access the force that directs all living entities in this world.

Let me emphasize that you can't merely pick up, say, a verse from the Gita and superimpose it onto your situation; you need to invest your intelligence and intuition so that you can receive its wisdom. That's how we win some battles and lose a few to eventually win the war of life.

Treat yourself to the knowledge that is abundantly available. Now, while you hear and study the scriptures, there are certain values that you can cultivate, especially since setbacks are usually round the corner! Chapter 6 discusses the importance of adjusting expectations and facing a crisis cheerfully.

SUMMARY

- Practical solutions aren't always the answer; abstract principles are also crucial.
- Scriptures don't provide short cuts; rather, they assure inner growth if we study them deeply.
- Scriptures help us hear our own inner voice.
- Many examples in nature point to a force that directs the wanderings of all living entities. When we listen to this 'wisdom', we access that force.

CHAPTER SIX

Facing Challenges like a Lion

'Don't succumb to helplessness – give up the weakness of the heart and rise, O valiant one.'

– Bhagavad Gita (2.3)

WHEN A HERD OF elephants passes on one side of the river, a pack of dogs on the other side will not dare bark at them but run away instead. But a lion or even its cub will not fear an elephant; he is, after all, the king of the jungle.

A sincere spiritual aspirant has to have the spirit of a 'lion' within, for when temptations or failures confront him he has to be able to face them. It's one thing to give eloquent discourses on how to face difficulties in life, but when this world knocks us down with heavy blows, most of us abandon the spiritual path. It needs great courage to face life's challenges. Your ability to face disappointments without getting discouraged determines your growth as a spiritual 'lion'. Two things are critical to develop such a spirit, as enumerated below:

ADJUSTING EXPECTATIONS

The first step is to change your expectations of others. We can't live in a utopian world free of troubles and misunderstandings. This world is what it is, often harsh and unsparing. If we are honest about our spiritual 'level' and realistic about the nature of this world and its inhabitants, we are less likely to be shocked when things don't measure up to our expectations. That's not to say you become pessimistic. You should hope for the best, yet prepare for the worst.

DAILY PRACTICES

The second step is to ensure your spiritual practices stay strong. A daily mindfulness practice of chanting, praying and service keeps your spiritual batteries charged.

The combination of adjusting expectations and mindfulness techniques keeps one strong and guarded, like warriors who train regularly. They work hard and sweat it out not because they want to fight a war daily but because they want to be ready at all times, and they know that the more you sweat in peace, the less you'll bleed in war.

Similarly, the material world is the antithesis of your spiritual existence. To expect freedom and eternality in the sphere of death and bondage is pure fantasy. However, the mindful and consistent practice of hearing and chanting helps you remain grounded, and to bravely face unexpected challenges. The chanting of God's holy names develops your spiritual muscles. Prayers help you see through the harsh winters of life.

Those who don't know how to tolerate suffering are generally the most miserable. Often the only right thing to do during suffering is to tolerate your troubles as quietly as you can until a better day comes around.

CRISIS HELPS MAKE CHARACTER

An old Bengali saying goes like this: If you want to look at a prostitute, you should see her early in the morning. That's when all the synthetic she put on the previous night has withered away. In the morning, she's devoid of her glamorous looks and makeup.

Likewise, if you want to see a person's real character, see how he faces life when nothing seems to be going his way. When life is in control, it's easy to be courteous and respectful to others, but how you choose to respond when you are insulted or misjudged, when you're down and out, or face failure, reveals your true nature.

Let's get an accurate understanding of life. If we expect our lives to always be easy and comfortable, trials will seem impossible to overcome. However, if we accept that we will encounter tribulations in life, we will be able to deal better with the things that come our way. And if we keep our spiritual practices strong, we will definitely find diamonds even as life throws stones at us. And that's a real lioness, marching on bravely, regardless of the odds stacked against her.

How can you improve your ability to tolerate suffering? The next chapter shares the tool of sharing and giving to charity.

SUMMARY

- Be more realistic in your expectations by hoping for the best and preparing for the worst. Daily mindfulness practices will help you tolerate suffering and energize you so you can fight life's battles.
- A person's character is revealed during times of crisis, not during the good times.

CHAPTER SEVEN

A Billionaire Renunciant

'If I am not satisfied with three small steps of land, I won't be happy even with a continent, for if I have one, I'd desire to get the others.'

– Srimad Bhagavatam (8.19.22)

OFTEN WE IMAGINE THAT money and material security will make us happy in this world. This chapter shows how us it is possible to be rich even with very little.

A news item on CNBC caught my attention once: Warren Buffet had given away more than $46 billion in charity since 2000. The chairman of Berkshire Hathaway hadn't taken a salary hike for the last three decades, and had also paid back company expenses such as phone charges. Buffet lived in the same house he had bought in 1958, and said no to all things hedonistic. I wondered if Warren Buffet was a renunciate in disguise!

HUMAN LIFE IS A LIFE OF RESPONSIBILITY

Although Buffet's motivation for giving up so much isn't clear, his refusal to pursue the 'I get what I want' lifestyle – the hallmark of modern society – comes as a breath of fresh air in these times.

The Vedic scriptures praise the glory of not (artificially) increasing personal wants.

'Everything animate or inanimate that is within the universe
is controlled and owned by the Lord. One should, therefore,
accept only those things necessary for himself, which are set
aside as his quota, and one should not accept other things,
knowing well to whom they belong.'

— Sri Isopanisad, mantra 1

When we recognize the proprietorship of God and contribute our little worth in ensuring that the needs of all are taken care of, we lead a life of responsibility. A life centred on acquisitions, gross and even subtle aspirations, for name and fame will only increase your bodily misidentifications. For such a person, a deep sense of insecurity crops up with changing conditions, be they twists in political fortunes or crashing stock markets.

Srila Prabhupada often exposed the latent fears and wild pursuits of modern man with this observation:

> According to nature's arrangement, living entities lower
> on the evolutionary scale do not eat or collect more than
> necessary. Consequently, in the animal kingdom, there is
> generally no economic problem or scarcity of necessities. If
> a bag of rice is placed in a public place, birds will come to eat
> a few grains and go away. A human being, however, will take
> away the whole bag. He will eat all his stomach can hold
> and then try to keep the rest in storage…This collecting of
> more than [is] necessary is prohibited. Now the entire world
> is suffering because of it.

THE ETERNALLY DISSATISFIED MIND

Besides social responsibility, another reason why we need to keep our lives simple is the personal satisfaction it guarantees. The more we gratify our desires, the more the mind continues to remain dissatisfied. 'There's enough in this world to meet everyone's need,' said Gandhi, 'but not enough to meet even one person's greed.' The human mind is fickle, and if we let go of its control, it shall know no peace. As we unleash our passion for acquiring different pleasures, the mind only points out the delights we haven't acquired yet. And the more elusive these delights are, the stronger is the desire to possess them.

The enjoyment of all things material follows the law of 'diminishing marginal returns', with the pleasure derived from each successive object or person reducing in greater proportion. A drastic gap occurs in the expectation of pleasure and the actual enjoyment experienced. To fill this gap then, the mind desperately urges us for *more*, to spend more, buy more, eat more, drink more. In the ensuing race for happiness, the mind's demands remain eternally unfulfilled. It's like scratching an itch – the more you scratch, the greater the itch. Repeated scratching finally leads to agonizing pain and bleeding.

CONNECTION TO GOD: THE SECRET OF SATISFACTION

'He who is content is rich,' said the wise Lao Tzu. When we lead a God-centred life, with a culture of prayer and service as the essential foundation, a sense of serenity fills our lives. The restless mind which pushes us to 'get what I want, when I want' is replaced by a desire to improve the quality of our offerings to God.

The mind's primary function is to 'like' and 'dislike'. The constant acceptance and rejection by the mind ensures that we are never peaceful and happy. The connection to God – known in various traditions as Krishna, Allah or Jesus – however, helps us transcend the petty mind. The relationship happens through chanting, listening to scriptures, service and prayers. Our spiritual happiness only increases with the passage of time, and simultaneously the craving for material possessions fades away.

THE WEALTH OF A POOR BANANA-LEAF SELLER

Over five hundred years ago, there was a poor banana-leaf seller who lived in the countryside of Bengal. His name was Kholabecha Sridhar. He was happy to offer half of his earnings to serve the Lord, and spent his time blissfully chanting and hearing God's name. Lord Chaitanya was impressed and revealed His supreme majesty in front of the poor man. He then asked Sridhara to ask for any benediction he desired. The banana-leaf seller said he only wished to remember the Lord and engage in loving devotional service.

Similarly, King Ambarish, during a previous time cycle (millions of years ago according to the Vedic calendar), was an ideal example of a king who possessed the wealth of God's consciousness in his heart. He used all of his senses and wealth in the service of his dear Lord Krishna. He is considered a renunciant because renunciation doesn't necessarily mean giving up everything; rather, it means using everything for the right cause.

A HIGHER PRINCIPLE OF POSSESSION

We can't renounce entirely, because the moment we possess nothing we cease to exist. A living being renounces something only to gain something more valuable. A student may abandon childish activity, or a servant may give up his job, but they do so for a better opportunity. Similarly, a spiritual seeker renounces the material world so that in exchange he gets something of spiritual value. He loves God and knows that everything belongs to Him. He therefore uses everything he has in the service of his beloved Lord.

Srila Prabhupada encouraged us to use all physical facilities and modern amenities, not for our personal use but to glorify God and to serve His children. Service is real renunciation because through this act we renounce the deep-rooted conception of being the enjoyer and proprietor in this world.

MAKING THE RIGHT CHOICE

If you find an unclaimed wallet, filled with 2,000-rupee notes, you have three options before you. First, you can keep it; after all, finders are keepers! The second choice is to 'renounce' the wallet, that is, put it back where you found it. These two choices involve the 'enjoyer' and 'false renouncer' respectively because the wallet doesn't belong to you anyway. The third action is to find the owner's address and return it – the more responsible choice.

Similarly, a devotee refuses to exploit the resources of nature for selfish enjoyment. He also does not artificially renounce things of this world, because the world and its resources are not his property to begin with; they belong to God. He therefore engages his wealth in the service of God while giving up the sense of false proprietorship.

A BILLIONAIRE MONK

Just like a billionaire can be a renunciant, a poor monk can also be a billionaire if he possesses and gives his 'wealth' in the form of service.

I know a monk who has been in the ashram for over two decades now and does plenty of regular services. It's not that he can't do anything better; he's one of the presidents of our ashram and is renowned for his classes. Still, he cleans the temple hall early each morning and washes all the thousand-plus dining plates after the Sunday festival, whilst also resolving conflicts, chairing the management body and writing editorials for the monthly periodicals and magazines the ashram prints. No wonder he's one of our most respected and trusted leaders, for he leads from the front.

Once, he had an urgent meeting to attend and missed his Sunday plate-washing routine. The next morning, a junior employee demanded an explanation from him. I was amazed to see the leader unperturbed at a junior member chastising him.

What amazed me more was his excitement later. He joyfully exclaimed that his service was now successful because at last he had been treated like a true servant, which he claimed was his real position.

While appreciating him for internalizing the principles of selfless service, I recollected Radhanath Swami's description of Ghanshyam Baba in his memoir, *Journey Home*. Radhanath Swami found his heart irresistibly drawn towards Ghanshyam, a small thin man in his seventies whose life and soul was dedicated to serving God and devotees day and night. He would offer everything he had to serve young Richard (Radhanath Swami's name before he became a monk) while continually saying, 'I am your obedient servant.'

Ghanshyam insisted on serving his rotis to Richard while starving himself. With palms folded, he said that the only thing he possessed was his service to all. He gave away his blanket so that Richard could sleep comfortably in the cold Vrindavan winter. Radhanath Swami wrote that his heart was deeply affected by this devotee. Ghanshyam wasn't a learned scholar, a business baron, a famous guru or a mystic yogi; but he was a real saint, his humility an expression of his love for the Divine.

We can therefore take the principle of charity, or the principle of giving up, a step further. You could be the impoverished Kholabecha Sridhara or King Ambarish, or someone in between – like my temple president – but you can still be a great renunciant by merely possessing God and seeing everyone else as your master, worthy of receiving service and love.

While businessmen may give charity with a hidden agenda, real happiness comes from service with no strings attached. But is that practical? Let's see the technique of 'higher taste' in Chapter 8 that helps us give without expectations.

SUMMARY

- Warren Buffet's example highlights the need to move from 'I get what I want' to 'what is my responsibility?'.

- The example of Kolabecha Sridhara and King Ambarish shows how a simpler life guarantees personal satisfaction.
- Renunciation doesn't mean giving up; rather it's about using money and other possessions for the right purpose/cause.

CHAPTER EIGHT

The Pleasure of Giving

'We suffer because we abandon real happiness of the soul which comes by selfless service.'
— Srimad Bhagavatam (10.70.28)

ONCE, ON A 10-HOUR flight to London, I rose sleepily to go to the lavatory. The plane was quiet; most passengers were asleep or watching in-flight movies. My stupor vanished as I overheard a stewardess at her station swear at the 'animals' on her flight. Later, as we disembarked from the plane, I thought about what had happened. The air crew serve their passengers, but is service really their motivation or do they work merely to earn a living?

The service industry caters to the needs of millions daily, but are we really serving others on this planet? Most of us are motivated by self-care, self-growth and our own happiness, which is undoubtedly a legitimate need. Nonetheless, for inner peace, we need to enter the spirit of service and not just use it as a tool for gain. Any meaningful relationship thrives in a space of genuine service. If people serve each other only because of what it gives them, it will not fulfil their hearts as much as when service is offered with the genuine desire to please the object of service.

Service has two sacred features: It is not only the basis of our internal happiness, but also our natural position. Whether it's the politician serving the country or a master caring for his pet, it is the spirit of giving and offering service that keeps the relationship going. Unfortunately for those raised in a culture where the gratification of the senses is glamourized, to think of others' well-being is difficult, and to be a servant always is inconceivable!

But just like artificial makeup in a drama stifles an actor and he feels relieved to take it off, similarly our positions as 'enjoyers' and 'master's is an artificial burden on the soul. When we genuinely give ourselves in service, we are dressed naturally. Bhaktisiddhanta Saraswati said, 'Once we decide to become a servant, we are relieved of the burning burden of being an enjoyer in this world.'

THE PEACE PHRASE: 'ALWAYS THE SERVANT'

Unlike the air hostesses I encountered, a villager taught me an unforgettable lesson in service.

At a small temple in the interiors of Bengal, I sat on the mud floor and softly chanted on my prayer beads. It was my day of solitude and reflection. The village was quiet and the temple had no visitors that morning. A lone elderly priest carried on his duties, softly humming a devotional song. After a few hours passed, he gently asked me if I would like to honour the food offered to the deities at the altar.

I was hungry and instantly said yes. As he took me inside, I wondered why he would want to feed a stranger. Indian temples and its priests had challenged my sensibilities often in the past, and the cynic within warned me: He knows you are from Mumbai, and he wants a handsome reward in exchange for the food.

As he enthusiastically served me second and third helpings of traditional Bengali cuisine, I decided to confront his demands later; for now, I was famished and this feast was a welcome break. However, I was alert and ready to negotiate with him.

As he happily trudged to the kitchen and brought forth more delicacies, I could see he was in his element. I wondered again.

Maybe he wanted a job in Mumbai for his son, or money or my shawl.

After the meal, I offered a small donation for his friendly services, and he dismissed it. 'If you want to give me something, I need one favour. Please don't say no to it.' I braced myself for what I knew was coming.

'Please pray for me and bless me so that I can chant and pray like you.'

'What?' I said, shocked at his response. I nodded and waited, but he said nothing more. Slowly, he folded my leaf plate and cups and silently cleaned the place. I asked him, 'Are you sure you want nothing else?'

'Oh, what more can you give me, son?' The elderly man looked at me with compassion. 'You have given me a wonderful opportunity to serve such a nice person like yourself. As for me, I am content living in this village. I have lived here for the last 70 years of my life. My sons take care of my needs. I need to express gratitude and give back to God and His children. Will you please pray for me and bless me?'

Now reality sank in. He merely wanted to give without expecting anything in return. Almost instantly I condemned myself for having judged such a noble soul. I left humbled but also deeply inspired.

I have met hundreds of people during my travels across India and it's not easy to remember all of them. But this man etched a permanent place for himself in my heart because he genuinely sought to give without expecting anything in return. In retrospect, if someone's devotion can move a sceptic like me, I wonder how the soft-hearted God feels when an act of sincere service is offered to Him!

CHANGING THE PARADIGM

Often we dwell on thoughts about why we are not happy and what we can do to find peace. We also wonder why others behave the way they do and why the world is in the state it is. For a day, let's change the paradigm; let's rise above the self and honestly seek another person's happiness. Ask yourself these questions: Can I bring joy to another person's life? Will my act make a meaningful difference to others? How can I best contribute? These questions can propel us to a spiritual level of existence.

A HIGHER TASTE

Raj, a friend of mine, often argued with me about the local trains of Mumbai. While I found the peak-hour travel disgusting, he exclaimed that it was all right. I probed him about the dense crowds, about how there's barely any space to even stand inside the trains. He looked at me as if I was crazy.

A few months later, he was transferred to a remote but scenic place in Assam. Five years later he returned to Mumbai. We again met often and had our friendly exchanges. One day, I casually asked him about his office travel and immediately he began lambasting the Mumbai trains. I was amused because I had previously seen him indifferent to the same train rides. Yet, now, he was expressing how sickening he found the experience.

It didn't take me long to understand what had caused this transformation in him. During Raj's earlier stay in Mumbai, he had no idea what it meant to inhale the fresh morning air or watch the beautiful sunshine fade at dusk. But when he went to an idyllic setting in remote Assam, he walked to his office and back home daily through verdant meadows, with the sight of exotic birds and beautiful lakes to fill him with joy. He experienced a 'higher' taste in life. When he returned to Mumbai's trains, the contrast was acute.

This experience helped me come to terms with why some people find a materialistic life centred on sense gratification normal. They feel that drowning themselves in liquor, drugs and the sensual passions of this world are the ultimate happiness. They question the rationale of rising early, serving others and chanting

God's holy names. But the puzzle is solved for one who, despite a past of sensuality, now takes to spiritual practices.

SIMPLE HABITS CHANGE US

After a few weeks of rising early, eating sattvic food, chanting, associating with spiritual teachings and offering little acts of service, our consciousness takes off to an entirely different realm. We experience inner contentment. The taste is rich and profound. Then, if we go back to an environment surcharged with the modes of passion and ignorance, we feel choked. The previous life of sense gratification appears gaudy and tasteless.

Daily habits of service can thus relieve us of our natural inclination to grab or exploit. While the service industry makes billions of dollars, it's only our service *attitude* that will bring us a billion dollars' worth of *peace*.

It seems natural to maximize our pleasures, but there are souls, like the priest in Bengal, who find it unnatural. For them, service is life. The joy of giving fills their heart with more happiness than the passion of grabbing.

That afternoon in the temple, I thought I had something and was guarding it. This man had nothing to possess and yet he gave me everything. I knew immediately that he was a wealthy man. His life echoes what Churchill said, 'We make a living by what we get; we make a life by what we give.'

What do we need to make this paradigm shift from enjoyment to service? And what will help us experience a better life? The answer is discipline and self-control, the topics for the next two chapters.

SUMMARY

- To rise above the self and seek another person's happiness is not some mental technique but a deeply satisfying experience.
- The service industry makes billions of dollars, but it's the service attitude that gives us inner fulfilment.

- Once we experience a 'higher taste' in habits, like rising early, serving others or eating healthy food, a past of seeking gratification appears unattractive.

CHAPTER NINE

The Quiet Power of Self-control

'Practise self-discipline under regulations; the Lord's blessings are then yours.'

– Bhagavad Gita (2.64)

WALKING FROM GOMUKH TO Gangotri in the Himalayan snow was an incredible experience. Over 20 years ago when I had trekked through these ranges, there were very few facilities for an overnight stay. In the small ashrams, the rules were strict – we had to rise early, and attend the morning and evening prayers. If you fell sick, you were accountable to the ashram's authorities. Amish, a friend of mine, had accompanied me. He struggled with the schedules but did not complain. When we returned to Mumbai a month later, he declared, 'I am glad I rose early. I can feel the difference in my consciousness; discipline is healthy and it has strengthened my mind.'

I met Amish and his family again in Mumbai, two decades after our rendezvous in the Himalayas. We relived our memories and flipped through old photographs. Amish was just out of college then; today, he is married and has two beautiful children. Turning to Seema, his wife, he said, 'Those few days of rigour and discipline were the best days of my life.' Then, as an afterthought, he looked at Seema and then turned back to me, and said, 'I am grateful I have a wonderful partner; she is my best friend.

Still, those days when I travelled with the monks and possessed no money, are most memorable. In retrospect, the austerity of a cold-water bath, living with simple wants and saying no to the pleasures of the senses is a heavenly experience. I saw self-control bring me immense joy.'

SELF-CONTROL BRINGS HAPPY REWARDS

Most people seek pleasures on the external, bodily level. Very few, like Amish, on that fateful trip to the Himalayas, choose to discover internal happiness that is not dependent on physical comfort. In fact, for many, even with a life-enriching purpose, discipline doesn't always seem exciting; it is rather painful. Later, however, you reap a bountiful harvest of honourable contentment. The road of restraint may be hard but the results are invaluable.

If you ask any successful sportsman or a student about their strict schedules, you'll likely hear them confess that the discipline is severe but the rewards are worth it. In the late 1960s, the Stanford University team conducted a series of studies on children by offering them a choice of one marshmallow if they ate it immediately; but if they delayed their gratification by 10 minutes, they'd get an extra sweet. Children who could wait longer for the rewards and practised self-control grew to attain more success in academics and relationships.

A disciplined lifestyle offers the same psychological effect as a large bank balance. A silent reassurance of money makes you feel safe – you know you'll have cash when you are in a difficult situation. Discipline acts in the same way; you feel safe and confident when you practise self-control. It is the solid support you need when you travel the distance from your dreams to your reality. You need to embrace discipline as a friend who gives you strength when you need it.

What makes champions different and successful is their determination to sacrifice distractions in order to achieve their purpose. Counter-intuitively, a denial of pleasure brings more happiness in the long run. A methodical lifestyle keeps us balanced and gives us a real sense of control over the mind and body. And with practise, self-control becomes more comfortable with time, especially when we remember what we want in life.

Living with distinct values may appear restrictive but is fulfilling. Life is more fun with rules. If you played football or cricket with no rules, would you enjoy the game as much as if there were challenges to achieve within the defined boundaries?

Even in your business, you may worry about your competitor's next strategy and lose sleepless hours, but Warren Buffet gave a simple formula: You don't have to be smarter than the rest; you just have to be more disciplined than them!

DISCIPLINE GIVES MORE FREEDOM

Temptations and distractions are many and relentless. We imagine that the freedom from temptation will bring us happiness. But this is like flying a kite: It may appear that if you cut loose the string, the kite is free from your control. The reality, however, is that the more dexterously you handle the strings, the higher you can fly it. Similarly, one may think that freedom from all rules and obligations is liberating, but when we balance our lives with the right kind of activities and restrictions, we can in fact soar higher.

Traffic rules and restraints help us drive smoothly. Imagine if there were no stop lights? Traffic jams and accidents are obvious guesses. Freedom, therefore, is not available in an unrestricted or indulgent lifestyle; instead, it lies in seed form, in your self-restraint.

BETTER RELATIONSHIPS

Recently, I helped a few friends resolve their differences. Their misunderstandings had grown deeper and I feared their relationship would end. The first day I mediated and in a desperate attempt to improve the situation I gave them many suggestions. At the end of the first round of meetings, we parted more confused and troubled than before. That night, I reflected on what went wrong. I realized that instead of trying to understand, I had listened with an intent to speak or give advice.

The following day, I listened to them without judgement – I restrained my urge to talk. Slowly, when I convinced my friends by my actions that I had understood them, I requested them to do the same with each other. One of them volunteered first to understand the others, resisting his natural urge to speak or get his point across. When the other person was satisfied that he was understood, it was his turn to do the same. And the mood changed from defensive to accommodative and then appreciative of each other.

The simple act of controlling our urge to speak paid such rich dividends during this episode. Imagine if we could practice these principles daily, what rich experiences would await us! John Milton reassures us in *Paradise Lost* with these words: 'He, who reigns within himself, and rules passions, desires, and fears is more than a king.'

DETERMINATION FOR A NOBLE PURPOSE

Some people practise strict self-control but only to delay gratification. When they stop pleasure pursuits artificially, the mind takes back what it was denied – with substantial interest. That's because saying 'no' to pleasures without a deeper 'yes' burning inside us is repressive and brings no real benefits.

Shaubari Muni was a highly self-controlled sage who meditated under the waters of the Yamuna. He wanted to avoid humans so that he wasn't distracted from his spiritual quest. However, he focused more on what he shouldn't be doing rather than the 'yes' within him. As a result, one day, when he saw two fish mating in the waters he was meditating in, his senses went wild. He went to visit a nearby king and married all fifty of the king's daughters.

Repression, the Bhagavad Gita, says accomplishes nothing in the long run (3.33).

Humans have a more developed intelligence as compared to other species. Therefore, it is our collective responsibility to not merely engage in sense gratification like animals do. Instead, let's follow austerities and discipline to purify our hearts. The Srimad Bhagavatam assures us that happiness that is transcendental to material pleasures is not only more virtuous but also continues forever (5.5.1). When we voluntarily embrace healthy rules – both socially and in our personal lives – we can ensure peace and harmony in this world.

Chapter 10 presents an alternative model of enjoyment that defies the power of time.

SUMMARY

- Discipline and self-restraint may not seem exciting now, but the rewards are wonderful. It is a choice you make between what you want right now and what you want in the long-term.
- Discipline gives more freedom.
- Shaubari Muni's story reveals that self-control alone won't help; one needs a positive purpose or intent as well.

The Race against Time

'Time I am, the great destroyer of the worlds.'
— Bhagavad Gita (11.32)

SIXTY-NINE-YEAR-OLD Emile Ratelband is struggling to attract women. Dating apps aren't helping this Dutchman, a motivational speaker, who has realized that younger women don't want an oldie like him. So he figures out a smart solution. He decides to legally reduce his age to 45! Easy, isn't it?

The BBC shared this bizarre story on 8 November 2018. 'Doctors say I have the body of a 45-year-old, I am a "young God", so I want to work, enjoy and date women while I can,' said Ratelband, as he initiated a case in a local court to change his age and improve his dating chances.

Life is a gift handed to us by a benevolent donor who'll eventually take it back. Like a stubborn child, I may wish to hold on to it, but he'll mercilessly snatch it away in any case. Instead of feeling gratitude for the fantastic gift I am bestowed with, I moan about the cruelty of it all. But haven't I seen death? Every week, I hear news about someone's death. He or she will be one among the lakhs of people who die daily on this planet. Or, to put it more graphically, every hour over 6,000 humans meet their Creator. Since you began reading this essay, over a minute ago, a hundred men and women would have died across the world!

We have all queued up to meet Time, but like goats in a slaughterhouse we are busy pawing the ground, chewing the grass and locking horns with other goats over trifles. Even as we inch closer to our end, we live in denial.

IS TIME AN ENIGMA?

Once, while flying from Mumbai to London, a passenger next to me adjusted his watch on our descent to Heathrow, and gleefully exclaimed, 'We've gained five hours.' I smiled at him as a contrary thought struck me: Our plane flew at around 700 miles an hour, but the fact that our planet hurries around the sun at 67,000 miles per hour (30 km/second), means we are always losing time – every second! My watch may stop one day, but time doesn't rest even for a nanosecond. At each instant, we are speeding towards death, yet our inability to ponder over this phenomenon, leave alone come to terms with it, is pitiable. We'll do well to remember what one philosopher said, 'Time is not bought ready-made at the watchmaker's.'

Let's say the court ratifies Ratelband's lawsuit and makes him younger. Would his life change for the better? Twenty years later, his body will be 90, but on paper, it's still 70. If he again desires to change his date of birth, would his body become that of a 50-year-old?

The cruel body clock cares nothing for our declarations and desires. Ratelband's story exposes a painful reality of the human psyche: An old man wishes to make the clock tick slower, while in youth we want time to move faster – our passion drives us to seek our ambitions and desires. But time is impartial and ever steady; it's a constant flow of grace, in perfect rhythm and harmony.

Time cares little for your rank or position. In death, a beggar will eventually meet a billionaire on a level playing field. The Italian proverb says it well: 'After the game of chess, both the king and the pawn lie in the same box.'

Meanwhile, hopes, if not transcended, frustrate us. With

advancing age, the capacity of the body to fulfil its never-ending cravings reduces. The widening gap between our fanciful expectations and the bitter reality of this world is what we often unknowingly refer to as stress or depression.

A HIGHER DESIRE: A LIFE BEYOND THIS BODY

'Never was there a time when I did not exist, nor you, nor all these kings; nor in the future shall any of us cease to be.'
— Bhagavad Gita (2.12)

Instead of racing against time, let's work on our aims and aspirations. Instead of contemplating how we can enjoy every moment of our time in this world, a more pertinent question to ask is: Why does everything deteriorate with time and is there a plane of existence that time doesn't influence?

To discover newer and deeper joys during our brief sojourn on this planet, we could begin to view life differently. Instead of thinking that we only have this one life and then plunge into gratifying our senses, let's consider our 70- to 90-odd years in this body as one part of the journey. You may catch sight of speeding cars outside your window, but you know they exist even before you glimpse them for a few seconds. And you know they'll continue to exist – honking and rushing – even after they've passed you by. Similarly, we live even after death; after all, the soul is eternal and beyond the temporary bodily situation.

Let's connect to the soul – our real and permanent identity. You may shed a tear or two while giving up your jalopy, but then you get a new car. The driver is different from the vehicle he rides. Our body is a rattletrap that'll eventually reduce to a bucket of bolts, but we have an identity beyond this. Let's seek it and we shall find it.

A CASE STUDY FROM THE BHAKTI SCHOOL

The Bhakti tradition reveals the potency of spiritual activities, where men and women, as they get older, relish more and more the process of hearing and chanting. Among many case studies, one that prominently stands out is the story of John and Roy, twin brothers from England, who set out in search of God in the late 1960s. They were in their mid-twenties then. After an earnest prayer at the splendid Blue Mosque in Istanbul, John was guided by forces beyond himself to dedicate himself to Bhakti yoga practices. John and his brother joined ISKCON, the worldwide mission founded by Srila Prabhupada.

Over the last five decades, John or Jananivas dasa, and Roy or Pankajanghri dasa, have quietly and happily served at a rural setting in Mayapur, 125 kilometres from Kolkata. When the brothers arrived here, they had to deal with extreme weather conditions and hostile villagers and dacoits who often attacked the temple complex where the brothers resided with other monks and members. Yet, the men served with untiring dedication, never leaving Mayapur even in the most trying circumstances.

The Srimad Bhagavatam says: 'Both by rising and by setting, the sun decreases the duration of life of everyone, except one who utilizes the time by discussing topics of the all-good Personality of Godhead.'

BHAKTI HELPS TRANSCEND TIME

The twins' absorption in service is contagious. Thousands who throng to Mayapur – now the world headquarters of ISKCON – can feel the enthusiasm, quiet grace, and spontaneous joy they exude so naturally. They have chosen to get out of time's clutches by changing their desires. While Ratelband desires to tell potential dating partners that he is younger than he actually is, the brothers convince everyone, without saying a word, that the Bhakti process can render you ageless.

The contrast that spiritualists like Jananivas and Pankajanghri provide exposes the paradox of our times. Many, like Emile, desperately want more time, but they use it in the worst possible way! Time is the one thing we all have in common; nevertheless, it's also the one thing that each of us uses differently.

The fifth canto of the Srimad Bhagavatam compares our life in this material world to that of a man who enters a forest to get honey from beehives. He accepts the risk of jackals, snakes and wild animals to get the honey. Finally, he also gets stung by the bees. Similarly, in this forest of the material world, to experience pleasure, one undergoes repeated suffering and pain from various sources.

LET'S CHANGE THE GAME

But we can decide to turn it all around. Before time eventually gets us, let's absorb ourselves in activities that nourish us. Each moment spent nurturing our souls is a significant investment we put in. Remember, if you lose money, you can earn it back. But every minute and hour we spend is lost forever. We can never get it back.

Let's graciously accept that Time is a school in which we learn, and it's also the fire in which we all burn. But before Time incinerates us, let's change and purify our priorities. With a spiritual purpose, we will face Time's verdict with honour.

What is the one thing that Time doesn't destroy in this world? The concluding chapter of this book examines the power of principles in this temporary world of birth and death.

SUMMARY

- With advancing age, the capacity of the body to fulfil our desires wanes.
- Time cannot influence our soul.

Choose Your Truth

*'All speculators must disagree with other philosophers; as
there are sages, so are the opinions.'*
— Yudhistir Maharaj in Mahabharata
(Vana Parva, 313.117)

The biting cold didn't weaken Deepak's spirits. As I reluctantly
trudged out of the hall, I overheard him singing prayers. His
buoyant mood was the antidote for the misery I felt at waking
up at four a.m. While the world outside our small ashram slept
blissfully, we had to rise early, have a cold shower, and perform
our spiritual duties. Often, I'd catch my mind protesting at this
regimen. As a new apprentice in the ashram, I had no choice, but
our tight schedules and rigid discipline all seven days of the week
tired me out. My heart yearned to lie on my soft bed at home
where I could rise four hours later, and no one could tell me to
do otherwise. But here I was, a monk in the making, and it had
all been my choice.

Deepak's sparkling and grateful temperament brought joy to
many. His cheerful humming early in the morning was an open
declaration that a monk's life can be a joyful experience. As I
returned from the shower and dressed, I spoke to Ashok about
Deepak's positive attitude, and how his absorption in our spiritual

practice was a great inspiration. I hoped Ashok would affirm my observation, but he stunned me with a sharp response, 'Oh, that's nothing. He had been down with severe constipation for the last two weeks. Now that he has been able to relieve himself, he is singing a happy song.'

I stood confused for a moment. What was the truth – my analysis or his judgement?

The wise Aki passed by me. He had heard us, seen my bewilderment and also expertly read my mind. He gently tapped my shoulder and declared, 'It doesn't matter what the truth is; what's more important is what you choose to accept.'

Later, I reflected on this. Perhaps, Deepak's happiness was transitory and he was happy because he had just cleared his stomach and wasn't as spiritually advanced as I thought. Nevertheless, was my appreciation false? There are others who aren't constipated, but they never sing a happy song. Wasn't Deepak special, like everyone else in the monastery? And by choosing to remember his unique quality of gratitude and simplicity, I had invited happiness in my own heart.

THE MANY WAYS OF SEEING REALITY

I once saw a drawing of an old woman that appeared to be that of a young lady when viewed from another angle. The way you see a situation could be different from the way your best friend or spouse sees it, and yet both of you could be right! But if you insist that the way you see things is the only reality, then not only do you miss the beauty of another perspective, but you also risk losing your relationships with others who view the situation differently. Truth, therefore, in this world of temporariness, is a relative phenomenon. Everything is in a constant state of flux in this world, and to insist that Deepak's bowel clearance alone caused his happiness would deprive me of another perspective – that of his goodness.

Deepak surely has human frailties, like each one of us has, but isn't he also made of a billion impressions, a zillion desires, and the potential for unlimited excellence? Isn't he another divine soul, a spark of God, with immense power and potential? To search for the 'truth' in each situation would then be foolhardy at best and arrogant at worst. Isn't it better to choose an aspect of Deepak's personality that will enhance our lives and encourage him as well to explore his divinity?

Can we ever find the truth in the matter that manifests temporarily to our vision in different forms? To discover it, we need to go beyond the temporariness of the visible world and connect to something that is eternal. And one phenomenon that comes close to the truth are 'principles'.

PRINCIPLES VS. VALUES: THE TRUTH IN A FALSE WORLD

Stephen Covey in his book *The Seven Habits of Highly Effective People* gives us an example of the law of gravity – an objective reality that, as a principle, doesn't change. Values, on the other hand, are subjective and personal. Even a robber who loots innocent people may have the value of never eating alone or may share his bread with a needy person. Values can differ for each person and change over time. Twenty years ago, I valued associating with my friends, whereas today I find solitude helps me connect better with myself. I still value meaningful friendships, but I value being alone daily for some time. Principles transcend age, time, place and people. Humility is a principle, and so is kindness – you accept these laws and reap benefits or ignore them and invite trouble into your inner world.

The more we connect to our principles, the more we are able to access the eternal space – the area of truth that's not affected by changes. In Deepak's case study, the choice for me was to connect with the ageless principles of gratitude and appreciation or to ignore these principles. In this situation, the benefits of the choice I made were obvious: When I connected to the principles,

I transcended the daily superficial wrangling of the mind that is usually absorbed with petty issues.

The lesson I learned from Aki (and that I followed in Deepak's case) is that whenever confused, ask yourself this: What is the principle at play here? Remember the principles don't change, but we do. If we choose to connect to a principle through appropriate action, we can discover a level of existence and fulfilment despite our daily humdrum routine.

The changing versions of this world don't matter. Principles are a far higher reality.

OUR DAILY CONTRASTING CHOICES

Twenty-five of us once travelled from Mumbai to Mayapur. Our journey involved a flight to Kolkata, a sumptuous lunch at the airport, and then a drive through the winding roads of Bengal in an air-conditioned bus. Finally, 11 hours of travel later, we reached Mayapur, safe but restless and hungry.

A day earlier, another group of 20-odd members from our congregation had travelled to Mayapur but they had done so by train and were exposed to the blazing heat. Further, their train was many hours late. Their delay alone was the total amount of time we had travelled! Besides, during the journey, they had no proper food – the cooked rice and vegetables had spoiled due to the heat. The train's bathrooms ran out of water as well. From my comfortable room in Mayapur, I had called one of my friends on the train and learned about their arduous journey. Finally, after six more hours of swerving through the potholes on the village roads, they arrived at Mayapur a good two days after leaving home.

Although I was sorry that they had to suffer so much, my initial sympathy transformed to awe and humility when I saw their attitude. My friend explained to me on the phone, 'Yes, the journey is difficult right now, but we are in good spirits.'

'How about the elderly and the children?' I asked, remembering an aged woman who had recently undergone a knee transplant and was travelling with them.

'She is cheerful and has been telling stories all the way. We sang and chatted all the time – it's blissful.' The loud laughter and banter I heard in the background convinced me that he wasn't merely putting up a brave front; they were all genuinely in a positive frame of mind.

Later, we met at Mayapur, and I said to the senior lady, 'But I am still sorry you went through this.'

She said, 'We are extremely grateful that the kind Lord has allowed us to visit Mayapur. Despite everything, we are here. Isn't this a great cause for celebration? Besides, due to heavy rains and the technical problems on the rail route, 36 trains got cancelled, but ours just got delayed. I dread to imagine a cancellation, for then we wouldn't be here at all. Moreover, we bonded with each other on the journey as we had real and not virtual chats.'

I asked myself what the truth was in this episode – the uncomfortable train situation or the happy experience of the travellers?

External situations are sometimes not in our control, but the choice of thankfulness in our internal world is entirely ours. And this is not living in denial, but merely accepting the inevitable and choosing an aspect of truth that helps our souls grow spiritually. A life of appreciation and principle-centred living is a higher reality as it helps us transcend the inhibiting laws of this world.

Vedic wisdom assures us that this attitude is the launching pad to travel from the temporariness of this world to a dimension of satchitananda – eternity, knowledge and bliss.

SUMMARY

- The same situation – Deepak's singing – was perceived differently by two people because truth is relative. Hence, our choice of truth is more important than the subjective reality.
- Principles are the closest thing we have to truthful living.

Values are subjective and personal but principles are always right; they transcend time, place and age. If we live by them, we will reap rich rewards.

- While external situations are beyond our control, the choice of gratitude (principles) is ours.

Practical Application

Mind Management

HERE IS A CONVERSATION between husband and wife:

'You don't love me!' screamed the wife.
'But I do love you and want to love you. Please help me understand you better,' pleaded the husband.
'You just don't love me, that's all,' she repeated.
The husband appealed to her again. 'What should I "do" that will help you "be" loved'?

Love is an abstract principle that makes complete sense to us when we also translate it as a verb. That's how all principles are – they resonate in two ways. First, just like the wife wanted to feel loved, we need to 'feel' it. Second, like the husband, we also want to see it applied in our daily lives, to know that it is doable.

The three principles of mind management – Awareness, Acceptance and Aspiration – are no exception to this rule.

FOUR STEPS TO NEGOTIATE WITH THE MIND

One day, I helped my niece resolve a dispute with her husband. I insisted that one of them needed to volunteer first to understand the other person. Only when your partner is satisfied that they have been understood are you allowed to explain your point of view. Although the exercise wasn't easy to apply at first – after all, we want others to do our bidding – they were able to understand one another with my prompting.

That day I realized the same method works when dealing with my inner spouse, the mind, whom I lovingly refer to in the feminine gender as 'Chanchal', or 'restless' in Hindi.

I follow four steps of communication with my mind:

1.   Awareness, being present in the 'now'
2.   Acceptance without judgement
3.   Negotiate with reason – connect with your Aspiration
4.   Acting with kindness.

Do you converse effectively with your loved ones? As you hone your inter-personal skills, you need to sharpen your intra-personal communication as well.

An examination of a recent pilgrimage I undertook may help you see the usefulness of these four steps of communicating with the mind (or Chanchal, in my case). Of the four steps, the first two deal with understanding the mind. The next two help the mind to understand one's vision and purpose.

STEP 1: AWARENESS IN THE NOW

I was restless, angry and in a terrible mood. My fight-or-flight response had been activated, and all this was happening at 3.45 a.m.

I had led a group of about fifty sincere spiritual seekers to Vrindavan, the holy town dedicated to Lord Krishna. It was the peak of the month of Kartik, when the temples are ten times more crowded than the rest of the year. I had told the group about the special early morning session in our temple, and how we could all experience it first hand at 4.00 a.m. They were excited about attending this session.

But now, at 3.45 a.m., I was in a wretched and hopeless state. I realized I had put my foot in my mouth. I was allergic to crowds and I knew several thousand devout pilgrims would attend the early morning session. I felt abused, like I was a victim, for I didn't want to go to the temple. I was doing something I didn't want to do. Where am I; what am I doing and why am I doing this? Nothing made sense to me.

I decided to follow the first of the four steps.

Yes, my dear Chanchal, what do you want? Let me understand you. As I stopped to connect with my mind, I instantly improved my awareness; I had taken a step back to observe my mind. Awareness of what is happening in the present moment is the first step in mind management.

To improve any relationship, you have to first understand the other person. When I pause to spend time with Chanchal, she is relieved. The mind has been heard and acknowledged, and this is very important because it's in the 'now'. I am not trying to understand what the mind wanted yesterday or may want tomorrow. I am not going to the past or future – I am here, now.

This is a big respite for Chanchal – and, interestingly, also for me. Her rant slows down. And since my being is integrated with hers most of the time, this awareness improves our bonding with each other. I am now able to live in sattva, and possess clarity and an inner sense of control.

(I recommend you read again the first two chapters of the 'Awareness' section where the three energies and the inner dilemmas are explained. That will help you recognize the dynamics of the mind better.)

STEP 2: ACCEPTANCE WITHOUT JUDGEMENT

I don't want to chant my prayers now. Chanchal is yelling at me in panic as an endless stream of men and women throng the temple courtyard. *I want to go back to my room and sleep. Let's go back to Mumbai. To hell with all these prayers, this damn spiritual thing doesn't work.*

I was slipping into quicksand. I could castigate my mind thus: *You rascal, what would the members, who look up to you as a teacher, think about you now? You are a hypocrite; you give big sermons and avoid coming to temples yourself. Wait till they find out.*

But I did not reprimand Chanchal. Poor thing, she was in pain, and if I instructed her, I'd be breaking a sacred principle of communication, which is to listen first and then seek to be understood.

I knew at this stage that I simply had to give confidence to my mind that it was perfectly okay to be who you are. *It is fine, I understand you and accept you* was the silent message I relayed to Chanchal.

When a batsman is hit by a bouncer, the worst thing fielders can do is sledge him – that could really break his confidence. When the mind is in pain, more negativity will only bash it further. It's not fair play in any sport. If you are hurt, fearful, or emotionally weak, don't lecture your mind on submission to lofty principles. None of them appeal to a mind that hankers to be understood, accepted and cared for.

(Chapters 2, 3 and 5 in the 'Acceptance' section will help you with keys to practise acceptance better. Chapters 12 to 14 share tools to support you slowly but surely in your journey forward.)

STEP 3: NEGOTIATING WITH REASON (CONNECTING WITH YOUR ASPIRATION)

After you've listened to the satisfaction of your partner, it is now ready to listen to yourself. When the mind is peaceful – and this happens quickly when it isn't judged – it is ready to understand yourself.

Your higher awareness – based on aspiration – guides you at this stage.

We've come to the most holy place of Vrindavan and these three days are special. Don't you want to get some of the Lord's grace in these prayer sessions? Won't it be great for us? Remember, we wanted to advance in our spiritual life.

Don't accuse your mind of being uncooperative – no slandering or chastisement will work now. Scathing remarks to your mind are just a way for your mind to reprimand your being, a way of entering your life through the back door. You can't escape the reality of your mind. Therefore, at the right time, let go of your obsession to control the mind. Just accept who you are and gently connect to your goals and vision. Add grace to make it natural.

The common mistake most people commit is that they jump to the third and fourth steps prematurely. You can't jump steps. First you have to empathize with the mind; only then can you expect the mind to cooperate with you.

(Chapters 2, 3, 4 and 11 from the third section 'Aspiration' can help you understand the need for self-care better.)

STEP 4: ACT WITH KINDNESS

I gently proposed to Chanchal: *Shall we stay near the western gate, way behind the rest of the crowd? That's near the exit, and in case you want to run away any time, it will be easy to leave.*

Did you notice that I suggested an action plan that honoured the mind's needs? My suggestion was to ensure that the mind stayed within its comfort zone. And to ensure Chanchal was happy, I actually went out a few times from the temple to inhale fresh air. *See? We are out and there's no pressure.* Here, I was being reasonable and kind. How could she refuse? After all, the mind, now vacillating and acting unpredictably, would later moan about missing the morning prayers.

Living only in the extreme, for example, having high aspirations, can break the mind. On the other hand, merely accepting ourselves and not improving ourselves can make us complacent, throttling our growth and learning. So the best solution is a middle path between one's aspirations and present reality. In the long run, one can tackle the mind better when one is sensitive to one's unique needs.

(Chapter 11 of the 'Acceptance' section talks of a healthy way to practise self-love.)

Since you can never really separate yourself from your 'Chanchal', why not make your relationship with your mind better? You have spent decades neglecting the needs of the mind, which is why the mind is now ruthlessly non-compliant and stubborn. Now it is time to try understand the mind. See the difference it makes to your inner world.

kindly offered me a place to stay comfortably and write this book. The officials at the Sanjay Gandhi National Park allowed me to explore the forest at odd times where, in an isolated corner, I found inspiration and answers.

My sincere thanks to Rukmini Chawla Kumar at Hachette India for taking on this book. She suggested relevant changes and helped me chisel the manuscript.

Mukunda Mala taught me how to use track changes and Microsoft Word, to write and edit better.

I feel indebted to my dear friends Abhishek Patil, Pawan, Nila Krishna dasa, Rahul Danait, Rasa Parayana dasa, Viki Chauhan, Sreyas and his mother Mrs Rajeshwari Iyer, Madhu Madhav dasa, Anant Raghav, Mohit, Vipul, Vaibhav, Mayur, Sridama dasa, Vrushank, Lalit Jain, Sandeep Shetty and many others for their constant support and good wishes.

My dad, mom, brothers, cousins, uncles and aunts have blessed me profusely. I owe a big thank you to each one of them.

My sincere gratitude to you – the reader – for picking up this book to read amongst a million other choices you had before you.

Acknowledgements

IF THIS SECTION WERE a thousand pages, perhaps I could mention everyone who helped me write this book, and what they mean to me!

My foremost gratitude to my spiritual master, His Holiness Radhanath Swami, who tirelessly taught me the various aspects of spiritual science.

I can never give enough thanks to Srila Prabhupada, a leading proponent of the science of Bhakti yoga.

My mentors, Govinda dasa, Gauranga dasa, Shyamananda dasa, Radha Gopinath dasa and Sanat Kumar dasa, for their patience and trust.

My friends, Gaurgopal dasa, Sikshastakam dasa, Chaitanya Charan dasa, Baladev dasa, Shivrama dasa, Sri Chaitanya dasa, Manohar dasa, Premkishor dasa, Radhika Vallabh dasa, and over a hundred-plus monks who teach me daily by their sterling example.

I sincerely thank Zayani Bhatt for her sharp observations, fine editing and kind encouragement, which helped this book take shape.

My deep gratitude to Suhail Mathur of Bookbakers.com who helped me get this work published.

Mr Maheshwari, Sri Raj Chopra, Krishna Gopal dasa, Gajendra Nath dasa and the staff at Gopal's Garden High School